Focus on Homelessness
A new look at Housing Policy

Edited by
John Blackwell/Stanislaus Kennedy

the columba press

the columba press

93, The Rise, Mount Merrion, Blackrock, County Dublin

First edition 1988
Cover by Bill Bolger
Typesetting and origination by
Typeform Limited, Dublin
Production editing by
Máire Ní Chearbhaill
Printed in Ireland by
Genprint Limited, Dublin

ISBN 0 948183 54 3

Illustrations:
John Blackwell, page 177
Michael Bannon, page 17
Focus Point, pp. 159,162,165,168,170,195

Photographs:
Rachel Collier, pp. 45,48,95,191
Royal Society of Antiquaries in Ireland, page 10
Derek Speirs, pp.11,29,31,37,40,55,63,65,69,77,81,85,91,
115,127,129,145,151

The publication of this book is sponsored by the
Department of the Environment and by Focus Point.

Acknowledgements

To the authors for their willingness to contribute to the *Focus on Homelessness* seminar and to this book.

To the Department of the Environment and Focus Point for sponsoring this book.

To the members of the Focus Point Social Policy Committee who helped, advised and worked on all aspects of both the seminar and the book.

To the staff of Focus Point and the Resource and Environmental Policy Centre, University College Dublin, for their help and contribution to the preparation of the *Focus on Homelessness* seminar.

To Dr. Garret FitzGerald for officially opening the seminar. A particular thanks to Professor Frank Convery who acted as seminar Rapporteur.

To the panel of speakers and all the participants at the seminar whose contributions are included here in "Recommendations and Summary of Discussion".

To the many individuals, all of whom should be named and cannot be, but who know the share they have had in this book and where our gratitude lies.

The *Focus on Homelessness* seminar was sponsored by Focus Point, Rank Xerox, the Electricity Supply Board and the National Rehabilitation Board.

The publication of this book is sponsored by the Department of the Environment and Focus Point.

John Blackwell
Stanislaus Kennedy

Contents

ILLUSTRATIONS

Introduction

John Blackwell/Stanislaus Kennedy

An historical perspective:
McGinnis Court, Dublin, 1913, and
The Liberties, Dublin, 1987.

The problems of homelessness, housing and housing policy raise major ethical, political, environmental, economic and social questions and concerns for everyone in society. This volume is a collection of edited versions of the papers presented at the Focus on Homelessness Seminar which was organised by Focus Point in the Riverside Centre, Dublin in January 1987, to mark the opening of the International Year of Shelter for the Homeless. It is not intended to be a comprehensive analysis of homelessness, housing or housing policy. However, this collection does bring together a wide variety of perspectives on homelessness and housing policy. The objective in presenting this diversity of views of those who make, analyse, implement and experience the effects of housing policies is not only to illustrate the complexity of the problems but also to develop a clearer understanding of the possible solutions to them. While the case studies focus on Dublin, many of the policy issues and principles have a wider relevance to the country as a whole.

The concept of homelessness is difficult to define and measure. Generally, people are thought to be homeless if they lack permanent residence and seek security and protection from the elements in shelters and hostels, bus stations, doorways, under bridges or squat in derelict or other premises. Homeless people are popularly perceived as being alcoholics, winos, vagrants, down-and-outs, bag ladies, oddities, lazy and no good.

This is, of course, a very prejudiced and narrow concept of homelessness. While a small and possibly *the most visible* minority of people who are out-of-home do have psychiatric and alcoholic problems and have spent much of their lives in hostels or sleeping out, the vast majority are people who have fallen onto hard times and wish to remain part of and live in the community.

In this volume persons are considered to be homeless if they are not only without shelter, but also without a home (i.e., a place where they belong, where they find peace and security), and if they are marginalised by the existing housing policy. It is evident from the book that homelessness is closely related to lack of co-ordination between the various Government departments and State agencies; to the lack of consultation with local communities and tenants; to the way in which the housing system as a whole operates. In the first section of the book we read how rapid population growth, pressure on land use and overemphasis on physical planning to the detriment of social planning in Dublin has resulted in division, segregation and even discrimination. We read how single parent families, young people and Travelling people are affected by housing policy and provision. All these groups experience the results of inadequate policy and provision; young people under eighteen years of age experience a total absence of policy and service provision; and Travelling people experience open prejudice, hostility and discrimination in both policy and provision. In this section also, we hear how people struggle against the odds to create communities and a better environment in the wake of bad planning and housing policies in Tallaght, Ballymun and the North Inner City. In all cases we are reminded how things could have been better if various groups and communities concerned were consulted and listened to before the plans were made or implemented.

In the second section of the book, representatives of various sections of Dublin Corporation and the Eastern Health Board describe the housing and welfare system and how it operates. While the authors do not deny the need for change, especially in the housing stock and welfare services, they all convey a sense of the improvements in housing provision services and their plan for the future.

In the last two sections of the book the authors acknowledge the changes and achievements pointed out in Section Two, but they emphasise that much more needs to be done, and describe how the causes and effects of homelessness have ramifications well beyond the provision and allocation of physical dwellings. Authors call for a complete review of public housing policy and provision and a review of housing finance policy in relation to public, owner-occupied, private rented and voluntary housing. Second, the potential for different types of housing, including non-profitable voluntary housing, is pointed out, as is the possible adaptation and efficient use of existing housing stock in the inner city. Authors call for the right of the individual to adequate secure housing at an affordable price to be acknowledged, and for special attention to be given to socially vulnerable groups such as young people under eighteen years of age, Travelling people, people leaving institutions and single parent families, all of whom have very little resources and means. While emphasising the importance of design in housing policy and planning, it is pointed out that no specialised *physical* planning or design is required for homeless people; their needs are as diverse as the housing needs of the general population. However, many people who are or have been homeless have special social and emotional needs which need to be considered, planned for and facilitated within their housing situation. People may require different types and degrees of support. This may mean facilities such as short or long term semi-independent living; shared flats; sheltered housing; community type housing and a wide range of settlement strategies and supports.

In view of the marked changes in housing circumstances and changes in population, family, social and economic structures and considering that we had no White Paper in Ireland since 1969, the conference participants called on the Government for a commitment to drawing up a White Paper on housing policy.

We are now at a major watershed in the history of housing provision and policy in Ireland. The great demand for new family housing has been drying up, while the social divisions in the cities are becoming worse.

What is clear from the authors is that any successful attack on homelessness and the problem of marginalisation in housing will rest on a number of factors. First, there is a need for society to grasp the severity of the problem in all its aspects, particularly the segregation, inequality and exclusion which present policies are bringing about.

Second, while the general improvement of housing provision in Dublin particularly over the past fifteen years has been impressive, this achievement

13

has to be seen in the context of a city where today, many individuals, groups, and communities experience the ill effects of bad housing policy and planning, and in which there is an ensuing sense of marginalisation, powerlessness and exclusion.

Finally, there is the need for the political will to formulate and implement policies aimed at the problem and not at its symptoms. This can only happen if the approach is coloured by the belief that adequate secure and affordable housing is a basic human right for every citizen.

During the period when this volume was being prepared, three changes in housing policy were announced.

- The £5,000 grant was abolished in the Budget of March 1987.
- Related to the fact that the Housing (Miscellaneous Provisions) Bill of 1985 lapsed with the dissolution of the Dail in early 1987, the Housing Bill, 1988, published in February 1988, is concerned among other things with homelessness.
- A more generous scheme for the sale of dwellings to sitting tenants was announced in February 1988.

These events do not invalidate the broad themes of this book; if anything, they make them more relevant than ever.

John Blackwell
Stanislaus Kennedy

What is the problem?

In this section Michael Bannon looks at the housing problems in Dublin as they have evolved in relation to the rapid growth of population and the pressure on land use in the Dublin sub-region. Housing problems in the sub-region reflect elements of the social structure and in particular the pervasive social segregation. The role which the physical planning process can play in influencing the settlement pattern is outlined. In this section also, the particular problems faced by single parent families are discussed, as are the problems of youth homelessness. The evolution of housing problems in three areas of particular concern – Ballymun, the North Inner City and west Tallaght – are taken up. Travelling people describe their own experience of housing policy. These chapters demonstrate that if high social divisions are to be overcome, major changes in housing policy will have to take place.

CHAPTER 1

Planning and social segregation in Dublin

Michael Bannon

Open spaces, though adequate in size, were poorly developed or maintained, and all too often there was a bleak, harsh landscape.

Introduction

It is now widely recognised that Dublin has grown more rapidly than any comparable European city over the past quarter century. The growth of Dublin has been fuelled through its own high levels of natural increased growth, through in-migration from the rest of Ireland and, in the 1970s, through the return of emigrants from abroad. By 1981 the Dublin sub-region had a population of between 1,003,164 and 1,091,903 according to definition.* By 1986 the population of the sub-region is estimated to have increased by approximately a further 2%. In the absence of any national physical/urban development strategy, the share of the national population residing in the Dublin sub-region has increased from 25.5% in 1981 to 28.9% in 1986.

The rapid growth experienced in the sub-region in recent decades has imposed severe pressures upon resources, land, labour and capital. It has also seriously challenged the ability of national and local administrations to plan or to develop satisfactorily on such a scale, especially having regard to our 'post-colonial traditions of individualism'.

Within the Dublin sub-region, most of the population increase has taken place within the built-up area as shown on Fig. 1.1. The population of this area has increased by 252,000 between 1961 and 1981 as shown in Table 1.1. The population expansion in the built-up area has been paralleled by a growth of its physical extent from 9,000 hectares in 1946 to 16,000 hectares in 1973 (Bannon, 1979).

Table 1.1. Population Growth of Dublin, 1951—1981

Year	Population	% change	% National population
1951	634,472	–	21.4
1961	663,389	+ 4.6	23.5
1971	778,127	+ 17.3	26.1
1981	915,115	+ 17.6	26.6

Source: Census of Population

Urban expansion in Dublin and in the adjacent authorities has been consuming in excess of 1,000 acres of land per year up to the mid-1980s.

The physical spread of Dublin is a reflection both of the city's overall growth and also of the thinning out of the population of older areas. Thus, the population of the inner city has declined from 269,000 in 1926 to less than 100,000 today, i.e., from over half of the total metropolitan population in 1926 to about one eleventh in the mid 1980s.

*The former number is based on the conventional definition of Dublin sub-region as comprising Dublin City, Dun Laoghaire Borough and Dublin County. The latter number is based on commuting pattern data as used in Eastern Region Development Organisation (1985).

18

Fig. 1.1 The Growth of Dublin.

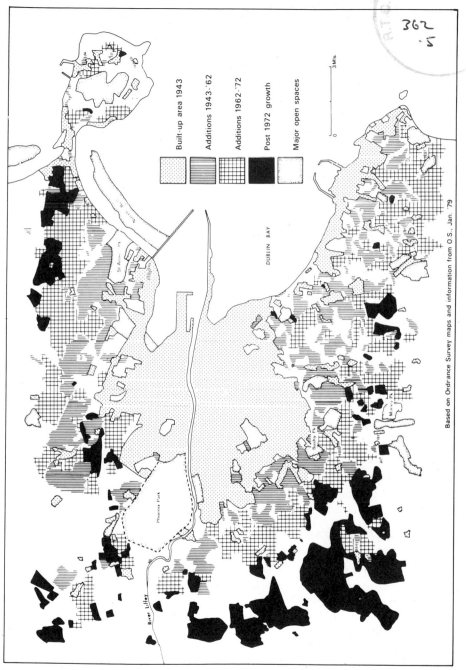

Source: Eustace and O'Neill, 'Urbanisation: Problems of Growth and Decay in Dublin', NESC *Report No. 55,* 1981.

Any continuation of the physical growth of Dublin will depend upon a variety of factors including the permitted density of development, the nature of the metropolitan housing policy and the priorities given to rehabilitation, renewal and infill developments. In any event, the recent dramatic changes in demographic and economic variables as shown by Blackwell (1985) (Fig. 1.2) suggest that Ireland is at crossroads in which new patterns of development may be desirable and in which new approaches to urban development are both possible and necessary.

Fig. 1.2 A Decade of Change – Demographic and Economic Variables.

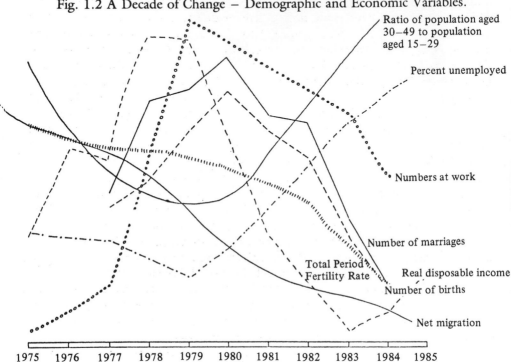

Source: J.M. Blackwell, 'The Issue in Perspective: Demographic Trends and Forecasts' in *Urbanisation,* An Foras Forbartha, 1985.

Social Structure of Dublin

To speak of Dublin in aggregate as a single entity is to mask many long-standing contrasts, divisions and even conflicts within its population. No population of one million people can be expected to be homogeneous nor would it be desirable that it be so. However, in the case of Dublin, social and economic contrasts are sharp and the social segregation of parts of the population has long been evident in the physical landscape of this city.

The social divisions in Dublin and their physical manifestation go well back beyond the nineteenth century. Thus, from Warburton's *History of the City of Dublin* (1818) we read of a city with:

20

spacious quays on both sides of the river . . . the squares and streets are, without exception, spacious, airy, and elegant, with every convenience that a city residence requires. As we advance westward, however, a gradual declension both in streets and houses is perceptible, . . . as we continue westward the scene continues to become more and more unpleasing, until it terminates in that neglected portion of the metropolis usually denominated the Liberty.

The writings of Friedrich Engels, numerous medical officers' reports and the findings of official inquiries testify not only to the perpetuation of these social divisions but to their intensification as tenements and the tenement population came to dominate the centre city in the latter half of the nineteenth century. The detailed report of the Departmental inquiry into *Housing Conditions of The Working Class in the City of Dublin* (1913) documented the nature of Dublin's social and housing problems – the implications of the flight of the middle classes, the consequences of failing to reform local government boundaries and valiant but hopelessly inadequate efforts of the voluntary and social housing agencies to meet Dublin's chronic needs. The evidence to the inquiry demonstrated that up to 60,000 persons required urgently to be rehoused and the report favoured a suburban solution for the most part.

In turn, this required a major investment in public housing and the erection of local authority dwellings on a scale never before contemplated. Despite the work of the Corporation, the problem of Dublin's housing was persistent – many of the tenements remained and by 1936 some "80,000 persons still lived in accommodation consisting of only a single room, including 25,000 in rooms shared by six or more persons. Nearly 2,000 insanitary basement dwellings were occupied as well as a large number of condemned habitations" (Horner, 1985).

By 1950, Michael O'Brien, the Dublin Planning Officer, estimated that 30,000 new dwellings were required to cater for the existing and future housing needs of the city (O'Brien, 1950). Indeed, the housing problem as inherited from the nineteenth century was to persist well into the 1960s.

Given the scale of the housing problem to be tackled in Dublin, several consequences were virtually inevitable. Attention was to focus on the provision of dwellings with little attention to individual requirements, housing environment or recreational amenities. Since large numbers of houses were urgently required, tracts of suburban land offered the cheapest, quickest and least complicated solution. As a result, housing infill, rehabilitation, joint arrangements with the private rented sector, the promotion of co-operatives or housing associations were all deferred pending a basic solution of the 'housing emergency' by the local authorities.

There was also another consequence. Just as the poor and deprived tenement population had come to dominate the social structure of many of the wards of the old city, so too the large scale, newly built local authority schemes at Marino, Crumlin, Ballyfermot, Artane, Finglas, Coolock and, more recently, West Tallaght were to perpetuate, on an ever larger scale, the social divisions so noticeable in the city of Joyce and O'Casey.

21

Despite the mammoth progress on housing reform, it was clear that by 1980 Dublin remained a seriously divided city and that the nature of the housing market had much to do with these divisions.

Measurement of Social Segregation

Social segregation can readily be observed on a qualitative basis, e.g., by various perceptions of the 'poor', the homeless, etc. More accurately, social segregation and by implication groups or areas of relative deprivation, can be quantified by reference to statistics on any number of individual indices – income, housing, employment, access to education, etc. In the case of Dublin, a number of studies has identified aspects of social contrast in Dublin using single indices – see the work on educational opportunity of Mac Gréil (1974) and the identification of educational priority areas (Breathnach, 1976).

But social composition and particularly relative deprivation is essentially multi-dimensional in character, and the use of single indicators tends to understate the extent and nature of such deprivation. Improved census data and the use of computer programs have enabled researchers to undertake a number of multi-dimensional analyses of Dublin's social structure and composition through the use of data on demographic structure, employment, housing and amenities. Brady and Parker (1975), Brady and Parker (1986), Hourihan (1978) and Bannon et al (1981) have all shown that Dublin can be divided into a number of 'social areas', each with its own problems and potentials. Thus, Brady and Parker (1975) mapped the wards of the built up area in terms of five major factors underlying social differentiation, while Hourihan identified seven social areas.

The study by Bannon et al mapped the 193 wards of the city using forty two variables to define six major social areas, each of which was further subdivided (Fig. 1.3). The characteristics of each of these six social areas are given in Table 1.2, which shows that of the six groupings, two were predominantly middle class and accounted for 40% of the total population in the study. These included older areas like Clontarf and Mount Merrion and newer private housing suburbs like Dundrum, Rathfarnham, Castleknock, Raheny and Howth. Two social areas could be described as transitional, area no. 3 characterised by multiple occupancy furnished flats, and area no. 2 a twilight one subject to social decline, disinvestment and rapid change. Typical areas included in the latter would be Fairview and Ranelagh.

There were two areas characterised by serious problems of deprivation – the inner city and area no. 5 embracing many of the newer local authority estates. Together, these two areas accounted for one third of the total population with recurring evidence of household overcrowding, low incomes, high levels of unemployment, etc. The inner city area in particular was characterised by limited incomes, an unskilled labour force, old housing and evidence both of over-crowding and of persons living alone.

22

Table 1.2 Characteristics of Social Areas and Sub-Areas in Dublin

Social Areas	Physical/Social Description	No. of Wards	Population 1971	% of Total Population	Most Distinctive Feature	Social Sub-Areas*
1. Inner City Areas	Areas of low income, multiple dwellings, suffering from acute social disadvantage	25	85,638	11.0	Multiple dwelling units	1. Lowest status area 2. Skilled, family housing areas 3. Private rented housing areas
2. Twilight Areas	Areas of older housing population	32	119,907	15.4	Widowed females	4. Terraced housing estates 5. Areas transitional to flats 6. Newer areas 7. Old, institutional populations
3. Flatland	Areas of multi-occupancy, (i.e. flatland)	27	97,671	12.6	Furnished flats	8. Older, furnished 9. Emerging flatland 10. High status flatland
4. Old middle class suburbs	Areas of older middle classes	24	75,452	9.7	Higher professional males	11. Southside high status areas 12. Northside high status areas 13. Newer high status areas
5. Local authority suburbs	Areas of local authority housing	37	173,006	22.3	Rented local authority housing	14. Older mixed tenancies 15. New estates 16. New flat complexes 17. Newer mixed tenancies
6. New owner-occupied suburbs	Areas of young and growing population	48	225,548	29.0	Households with greater than 6 rooms	18. Low status areas 19. Older, mixed areas 20. High status areas

*The title of each sub-area reflects its performance relative to its own social area, not to Dublin Metropolitan Area as a whole.

Source: Bannon, Eustace and O'Neill (1981)

Fig. 1.3 Social Areas in Dublin.

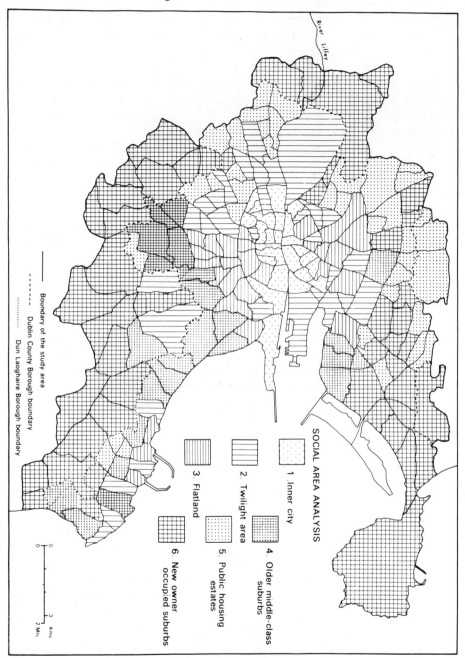

SOCIAL AREA ANALYSIS

1. Inner city

2. Twilight area

3. Flatland

4. Older middle-class suburbs

5. Public housing estates

6. New owner occupied suburbs

Boundary of the study area

Dublin County Borough boundary

Dun Laoghaire Borough boundary

Source: Eustace and O'Neill, 'Urbanisation: Problems of Growth and Decay in Dublin', NESC *Report No. 55,* 1981.

In the case of the local authority estates under examination, while houses were well constructed, in general they were too small for the resident population and incapable of extension. Gardens and open spaces, though adequate in size, were poorly developed or maintained and the result, all too often, was a bleak, harsh landscape. Basic neighbourhood facilities, telephones, shops, cinemas, unemployment exchanges etc. were often unavailable within reasonable distance. Access to necessary amenities and facilities was often difficult and costly. But the root problems lay in inadequate income and insecure employment which in turn were rooted in limited levels of educational attainment.

This survey was based partly on 1971 Census data and updated by way of household surveys carried out in 1979. This precise analysis has not been repeated with 1981 data due to lack of resources but Brady and Parker's analysis shows that the city's social class structure "has been relatively stable" (Brady and Parker, 1986).

Their analysis shows that social class differences give the city a highly segmented social geography and they point out that "social class differences expressed as variations in demand levels and disposable incomes affect not only the development of shopping and entertainment facilities but also the provision of public and private transport facilities." In other words the city is segmented severely in terms of housing and, thus, in terms of social class; this social segmentation is then widely reflected in income and expenditure patterns. There is little evidence of either social integration or any move towards economic equalisation.

Nor is the situation greatly different in the newer suburbs like Tallaght where neighbourhoods tend to be comprised of people in the same social class, and West Tallaght which exhibits many of the difficulties and problems which emerged in most of the older and larger local authority housing areas. Indeed, it is these newer housing areas which give urgency to the need for a reassessment of the role of public housing and of the relevance of physical planning in shaping our city and the environment in which we live.

The Role of the Planning Process

The picture that emerges of present-day Dublin is of a city conforming closely to the classic free market, segregated city model in which public policy has had an inadequate influence upon the paternity or composition of development. The highly segregated reality of the 1980s is an indictment of socio-economic policies which have failed to significantly reduce the class differences in society in the last quarter century.

These class differences have been heightened and made increasingly obvious through the very narrow focus of housing policy pursued over several decades. But most of all, this map of socially divided Dublin is abundant evidence that the physical planning process has, at best, limited influence over the investment decisions of either public housing departments or private developers.

Nor is it surprising that planning has had a limited influence when we examine the underlying realities in terms of both the aims and scope of planning. The aims

25

of physical planning are clearly threefold: aesthetic, economic, and social. In the case of Ireland, there have never been clear definitions of the aims of planning, of the order of priority between different goals or of the balance and interaction between the various aims. Thus, in the absence of any metropolitan-regional plan, much of the time of planners has been spent in development control, concerned largely with design considerations and architectural detailing. There is a need to examine the economic and social costs and benefits of much of this activity. One becomes increasingly distressed by architectural extravaganzas (for example the Quays, O'Connell Street) which pay little regard to the existing environmental context, the economic base of the area or the social consequences of such proposals.

But if physical planning is to play a greater and more effective role, then its scope and powers require to be strengthened.

In any society the scope of planning operations is determined by the following:
- The nature of the governmental process
- The legal supports for planning
- The extent of resources available, and
- The degree of public commitment.

In our representative democracy, implementation of plans is dependent upon the attainment of consensus. For planners, progress is made difficult since, while planning is vested in local authorities, power and control is increasingly exercised by central government. Moreover, Ireland has no national or regional physical development strategy. The legal basis of Irish planning is both limited and increasingly subject to negative control decisions rather than to positive development. There has been no reform of the planning structures in over twenty years and constitutional constraints result in preference being given to private rights over public and social needs under the Planning Acts. Under the present system, planners have little or no control over resources. Staff is limited, career structures truncated and access to decision-making often indirect. The planning department is not a spending department and must rely on the private sector or on other public sector departments and agencies to implement its proposals. Most seriously, twenty years of discussions have failed to produce any satisfactory mechanism for control of the price, ownership or ready availability of development land.

Too much of the planning process in this country is secretive and remote, with public participation being almost synonymous with protests about, or opposition to, specific local projects. The resources of public support and community development have largely been neglected.

Despite the dedication and commitment of individual planners, one cannot realistically expect the planner to have had a major influence on social patterns given his limited powers and the entrenched nature of social stratification within our society. The actors who are centre stage in the development process are landowners, investors, developers and the spending and executive departments of

26

local authorities, Government departments and State agencies. Planners and the planning process can influence some or all of these factors, but they have little control at the end of the day. Nowhere is this more evident than in regard to housing policies and especially housing policies pertaining to inner city areas.

The Development Plan and Housing

The five year development plan is the principal instrument of planning policy for each local authority. The attention to housing issues in most of these documents to date has been limited and confined to purely physical and land use issues.

Thus, the Dublin Corporation Development Plan (1980) included sections on recent housing construction, housing need, enforcement of aspects of the Housing Act, 1969, policies to protect and/or improve residential amenities, the specification of density, floor space and other related housing standards. Rehabilitation received minimal attention.

Similarly, the Dublin County Plan dealt almost exclusively with land use aspects of housing although there was reference to an objective to "prevent exploitation of the homeless" and also an explicit commitment to "provide sites for dwellings to be erected by persons of modest means".

For the most part, the traditional planning approach confined itself to the estimation of housing need which was then translated into acres of land required, given specified standards. Specific parcels of land were then zoned for housing and ancillary uses. Within this framework, the planner had little control over whether or not the land was used for public or private housing or for high or low income housing by either the housing market in the private sector or the housing department of the local authority. The Development Plan thus facilitated the public or private development to meet the housing needs as they perceived them and in a manner which they deemed appropriate. The planning role was to facilitate rather than to intervene actively. However, at the same time, planning in common with other public policies did impose increasingly stringent minimum standards which had the side effect of making marginal housing more expensive or else of taking such housing out of the market.

In addition, the limited powers of planners to control the spread of other uses also led to a reduction of housing accommodation, especially within central Dublin. Indeed, insofar as the Dublin City Plan of 1980 contained any social objectives, it is depressing to see how few of these have been realised.

Future Influence of Planning Policy on Housing

For the future there are indications that the planning process is becoming more socially concerned. Thus, a recent working paper on Dublin's Inner City provides both a realistic appraisal of the performance under the 1980 Plan and also contains positive and constructive analyses and discussions on the future of inner city communities, inner city housing, rehabilitation, conservation and the role of housing associations and housing co-operatives (Dublin Corporation, 1986).

27

Whether many of the laudable aspirations of the working paper can be translated into specific objectives and whether the planners can secure the implementation of such objectives will require major changes in both the powers of the planning department and the reform of the planning structures as they relate to Dublin.

Thus, in the NESC report on *Urbanisation: Problems of Growth and Decay in Dublin* (Bannon *et al*, 1981) it was proposed that the successful planning of Dublin required a two-tier statutory planning process, as follows:

1. *Strategic Plan* embracing the built up area of the city and its effective commuter hinterland. This strategic plan would involve participation by all the major interests investing in and developing the area and would be concerned with the laying down of broad guidelines for overall development. Such a strategic plan should be the subject of independent inquiry under the Minister for the Environment.

2. *Local Plans* would be prepared within the context of the strategic plans for community and neighbourhood areas and districts and involve a very high level of local involvement in their formulation and implementation.

It is through such local plans that local and special needs, local resources and local opportunities can be dealt with or utilised. At this level, groups and issues, which currently might be construed as a problem, can become a resource. At this level, and only at this level, can one put forward operational policies for social diversification, flexibility in housing construction, support for rehabilitation and conservation.

At the same time, local communities and local groups can form the basis for housing associations and co-operative initiatives. The hallmark of local plans is flexibility in responding to local and evident need. In this context the local planning process becomes the detailed framework for all public policy, especially for housing policy.

It is hoped that reform of local government in Dublin will somehow be revised to take on a satisfactory two-tier model at least to the point of enabling a statutory two-tier planning process to take place.

Conclusions

There have been numerous housing inquiries held to examine Irish housing needs. There have also been several White Papers on housing and Housing Acts. For the most part these have dealt solely with housing and confined themselves to the means whereby the output of the construction industry might be increased and/or the physical stock of housing improved.

In the 1980s the focus of the housing problem has changed in many ways. First, the nature of housing need has changed dramatically. The large need to provide for families on the waiting list has tended to be replaced by needs to provide for small families, single parent families and one and two person households.

Second, the narrow focus of the Irish housing system – almost exclusively public

Privately owned housing in South Dublin city. In Dublin, social and economic contrasts are sharp and the social segregation of parts of the population has long been evident in the physical landscape of the city.

rented and owner-occupied – has become the focus of growing criticism as such a system fails to encompass adequately the needs of present-day marginal groups. This dual system has helped to squeeze out the private rented sector. Moreover, for whatever reasons, voluntary, co-operative and local housing responses have been of negligible importance in the history of housing in this State.

Third, a major issue is that of the housing environment. In the efforts to deal with increasing the housing stock, little resources were devoted to other closely related issues such as the provision of facilities, the development of open spaces, the provision of recreational facilities, etc. These have now become of central importance and the problems arising from the past policies are considerable. Nor is it satisfactory to have one agency dealing with housing and others dealing with environmental and community issues at a later stage. We require comprehensive planning and execution at local plan level. It is not sufficient to have the Housing Department providing dwellings and then at a later stage, the Roads Department providing roads, the Parks Department taking over the open spaces and (in effect) no one adequately looking after employment, commercial provisions or social facilities in many instances. What is required is comprehensive local planning which phases in facilities in line with local needs. The housing budget should embrace the cost of the development of the residential environment.

Fourth, a major concern must be the consideration of providing facilities for local employment within neighbourhoods as well as the provision of proper neighbourhood facilities.

Fifth, an issue for urgent examination should be the effects of national housing policies at local level – e.g. the effect of tenant purchase and the £5,000 local authority grant.

Finally, there is concern relating to the inner city. Much good, attractive public housing has been erected in the inner city in the past decade and these developments have been good for the physical and social development of parts of the inner city. But public housing is not enough. If there is to be a White Paper on housing, then that paper must deal with flexible mechanisms to foster joint ventures in housing between the public and the private sectors, the promotion of co-operatives and the development of voluntary social housing. I would hope that the Paper would address sympathetically the role of the housing associations and that it would provide the means for a socially and physically comprehensive housing policy, especially for inner city areas, with a reasonable balance between new building, rehabilitation and conservation of the existing stock and fabric.

For the future, housing policy needs to work through local plans and local housing area plans which foster social integration and ensure a pleasant, stimulating and enriching environment in which to live.

References

Bannon, M.J., 'Urban Land' in D. A. Gillmor, *Land Use and Resources of Ireland,* I.P.A., 1979, Dublin, p. 250-269.

Bannon, M.J., Eustace J.G. and O'Neill M., 'Urbanisation: Problems of Growth and Decay in Dublin' in: National Economic and Social Council, *Urbanisation: Problems of Growth and Decay in Dublin,* NESC Report No. 55, Stationery Office, 1981, Dublin.

Bannon, M.J., 'The Changing Context of Developmental Planning', *Administration,* Vol. 31, 1983, Dublin p. 112-146.

Blackwell, J.M., 'The Issues in Perspective : Demographic Trend and Forecasts', *Ireland in the Year 2000 — Urbanisation,* An Foras Forbartha, 1985, Dublin p. 5-16.

Brady, J. and Parker, A., 'The Factorial Ecology of Dublin', *The Economic and Social Review,* vol 7, 1975 p. 35-53.

Brady, J. and Parker, A., 'The Socio-Demographic Spatial Structure of Dublin in 1981', *The Economic and Social Review,* vol. 7, 1986, p. 229-252.

Breathnach A., 'Towards The Identification of Educational Priority Areas in Dublin', *The Economic and Social Review,* vol. 7, no. 4, 1976, Dublin p. 367-382.

Dublin Corporation, *The Inner City,* Working Paper, 1986, Dublin p. 75.

Eastern Region Development Organisation, *Eastern Region Settlement Strategy* 2011, ERDO, 1985, Dublin.

Grist, B., *Twenty Years of Planning,* An Foras Forbartha, 1983, Dublin p. 18-19.

Horner, A., 'The Dublin Region, 1880-1982: An Overview on its Development and Planning' in: *The Emergence of Irish Planning 1880-1920,* ed. M. J. Bannon, Turoe Press, 1985, Dublin, p. 48.

Hourihan, K., 'Social Areas in Dublin', *The Economic and Social Review,* vol. 9, 1978, Dublin p. 301-318.

Mac Gréil, M., *Educational Opportunity in Dublin,* C.I.E.C., 1974, Dublin, p. 57.

O'Brien, M., 'The Planning of Dublin', *Journal of The Town Planning Institute,* vol. 36, 1950, Dublin, p. 208.

Warburton, J., et al; *History of the City of Dublin,* Cadell and Davies, 1818, London, p. 443.

CHAPTER 2

Housing policy as it affects single parents and their children

Mary Higgins

The type of accommodation on offer in the private rented sector is notoriously poor, with high density occupation, small space, inadequate and often shared facilities.

Introduction

The lack of a comprehensive housing policy which recognises the housing and related needs of single parent families, gives rise to many problems in their lives.

Almost all of the women who contacted Cherish in 1986 experienced some level of difficulty in relation to housing. The problems presented in 1986 were basically no different to those presented by women in 1973, when Cherish was founded.

The opportunities for solving these problems have changed and improved slightly over the years. Mother and baby homes now provide accommodation for some period after, as well as during, pregnancy; local authorities in most parts of the country will accept applications from, and house single parents; families are often more supportive to their daughters and will allow them to remain in the family home; rent subsidies for social welfare claimants living in the private rented sector are now available. However, single parent families have difficulties in acquiring independent accommodation which is secure and affordable, adequate for their needs, and which allows them to establish a basis for family life and share in the way of life of other members of society.

Lack of Choice

The difficulties experienced by single parent families arise mainly because of their economic position. Most single parents depend on social welfare and therefore have little or no choice over the kind of housing they live in.

For many single parents, this lack of choice and control forces them into situations which are neither adequate for their needs nor afford the security and independence which they require. In practice, the options for many single parents are limited to the following: remaining in the family home, live-in jobs, hostel type accommodation and shared accommodation.

Remaining in the Family Home

Remaining in the family home is seen by some as an ideal solution to the housing needs of single parents. It is very rarely an adequate means of caring for their long-term housing needs. Those women who contact Cherish, needing to secure alternative accommodation when the provision within the home has broken down, are frequently in considerable distress. Very few families have the physical space within their parental home to adequately accommodate, let alone foster the development of, two families. The child often becomes the focus of tension between the single mother and the grandparents. Disagreements arise about child rearing methods. Some grandparents feel so strongly that the care of the child is the mother's responsibility that the mother cannot go out at night and leave the temporary supervision of the child to the grandparents nor can she bring in a babysitter.

Other grandparents feel that they have literally been left holding the baby, with their daughter taking little or no responsibility for its care.

32

Live-in Jobs, Hostels and Sharing

Similar problems occur in the live-in jobs, hostel and shared accommodation and very often single parents are forced into seeking alternative accommodation. It is extremely difficult for a single mother and her child to establish themselves as an independent family in another family's home or indeed in any situation which is dominated by other people's rules and strictures.

Housing Needs

The housing needs of the single parent families in contact with Cherish are clear. They need adequate, secure permanent accommodation at a price they can afford. The extent to which these needs are met in the different housing tenures is now discussed.

Local Authority Housing

Although local authority housing is becoming a reality for more single parent families than in the past, current provision and letting policies in this sector rule it out as a viable option for many. There are a number of reasons why this is the case.

First, there is the lack of availability of suitable housing. Most housing schemes are designed to cater for the needs of two-parent families and do not contain units of accommodation appropriate to the needs of smaller non-expanding families such as a single parent with one child.

Second, the system of allocating points for housing on the basis of family size means that single parent families move very slowly up the list. This is partly because they compete with other expanding families, and partly because no account is taken of factors such as emotional stress and the particular tensions which can beset single parent families.

Some local authorities clearly consider the housing needs of single parent families to be less pressing than those of other groups, and single parents themselves to be less deserving than two parent families, disabled or elderly people.

Third, the restrictive application of residency qualifications operating in all local authority areas creates many problems for single parents. The housing needs of single parent families are often immediate and many will have to make frequent moves in order to solve them. In so doing, they may unwittingly move from one local authority catchment area to another and consequently fail to fulfill the residency qualifications required before they can even be considered for housing. This problem is particularly acute in the Dublin sub-region where people move between Corporation, County Council, and Dun Laoghaire Borough areas.

The end result of these difficulties is that many single parents simply do not bother to apply to their local authorities for housing either because they feel that they have very little chance of being offered anything at all or because they feel (with some justification) that they are likely to be offered housing which is in low demand because of its condition or because of its lack of accessibility to their jobs, families, friends or other support systems, means that they could not survive. In turn, this gives local authorities a deflated picture of the numbers of single parent families who require housing and who would accept housing if it were more accessible.

These difficulties are exacerbated by the fact that it is especially difficult for single parents to transfer tenancies from one area to another. It must be stated that many single parents have been housed by local authorities around the country and are quite satisfied with their housing conditions. It must also be stated that because of the availability of local authority housing in the last few years, Dublin Corporation area single parent families are housed more easily and quickly than in the past. However though their basic housing needs, in terms of shelter, may have been met, they are usually housed in 'low demand' areas. In these areas they are often isolated from families and friends. In most of these areas shops, recreational and other amenities including nurseries and public transport are few and far between. Thus, the problems facing these families may only have been transformed, not resolved, with a new set of problems arising. The experience of Cherish over the last year indicates that some women, in desperation, have given up their local authority tenancies, preferring to seek accommodation in the private rented sector.

The Private Rented Sector

The majority of women who are in touch with Cherish live in the private rented sector. Acquiring accommodation in this sector poses particular problems for single parents. Some landlords seem to think that they will upset their tenants or lower the moral tone of their properties if they house single parent families. The bargaining power of landlords in this tenure is quite strong in relation to that of tenants, as has been documented by Threshold (O'Brien and Dillon, 1982).

Landlords have often been reluctant to offer lettings to single parent families, whether because of a reluctance to let to families with children or for other reasons. Rents are very high in proportion to income and present particular problems to families who depend on social welfare and to working mothers who have the additional expense of day care (which costs about £30.00 per week). For social welfare claimants the supplementary welfare rent allowance does help to reduce this burden but the discretionary aspect of rent allowance causes problems for many single parents. For instance, the amount paid in relation to need can vary from one area to another, giving rise to inequities in treatment.

Moreoever, the type of accommodation on offer in this sector is notoriously poor, with high density occupation, small space and inadequate and often shared facilities. These problems are particularly difficult to cope with when young children are involved. Lack of security of tenure also causes great stress for parents who are faced with the continuous possibility of being given one week's notice to quit. For many women who look to Cherish for help, such problems as harassment, intimidation, evictions, legal or illegal, by landlords are not uncommon.

Hidden Homeless

Many single parent families are homeless but would not be officially considered as such. These are the families living with relatives or friends, staying in hostels or other temporary accommodation under threat of eviction, or living in other accommodation which is overcrowded or lacking in basic amenities.

They have shelter but could not be said to have a home or to be adequately housed. These ill-effects of the current housing situation on single parent families cannot be overstated. They can create feelings of despair and hopelessness among mothers. They undoubtedly create problems for children and heighten the chances of a child being admitted into the care of the health boards (not an unheard of response to an expressed housing need) which means extra cost to the State in terms of health and social services.

Conclusions

Housing policies have, in general, failed to make an adequate response to the housing needs of single parents. The problems encountered by single parent families in acquiring adequate, secure, permanent accommodation at a price they can afford are enormous. Secure accommodation can only become a reality for a single parent if she purchases her own home or manages to secure a local authority tenancy. Clearly the former is beyond the reach of the overwhelming majority of single mothers who simply cannot afford it and who do not qualify for loans. For those in the private letting tenure, little consideration is available and they are in a weak bargaining position. The tragedy is that many single parents are trapped in the private rented sector, with no possibility of organising enough money to purchase their own homes and never accumulating enough points to qualify for public housing. When single parents do acquire local authority housing, they tend to be given dwellings in low demand locations, where there is a concentration of single parents; this tends to increase their marginalisation.

An improvement in housing conditions for single parents depends on achieving an adequate response from housing policy as a whole to current problems. A comprehensive approach to housing policy is necessary if existing housing needs of single parent families are to be met. The basis for any future housing policy must be the recognition that everyone living in this country is entitled to adequate, secure accommodation at a price that he or she can afford to pay. Such a recognition will ensure that housing policy is based on need. A comprehensive housing policy should co-ordinate the public, private and voluntary sectors to ensure that a sufficient quantity and variety of housing is available.

New local authority housing developments must be designed on the understanding that the quality of neighbourhoods, access to amenities and opportunities for community development are as important as the quality and type of houses built. Consultation should take place with people who deal with the problems created by bad housing and more importantly, with the people who will occupy the houses. Local authorities should diversify their stock to ensure that the size, type and location matches the needs of people requiring it.

Subsidies for housing, both direct and indirect, must be reappraised so that resources can be directed more efficiently and shared more equitably.

In the short term, many of the hardships experienced could be alleviated by the introduction of legislation providing tenants in the private rented sector with some level of security of tenure. Access to local authority housing would be improved if the 'points system' and allocation policies took account of emotional stress suffered through continual mobility and insecurity. Residency qualifications should be abolished or at least made transferable allowing people to be considered for housing on the basis of need, rather than the length of residency in a given area. The enactment of the Housing (Miscellaneous Provisions) Bill, 1985 would provide people who are homeless with an entitlement to housing from local authorities.

In the medium term, existing subsidies for housing costs to low income households (differential rent schemes, social welfare rent allowances, supplementary welfare and rent/mortgage subsidies) should be replaced by a single housing benefit funded by central Government and administered by local authorities. It should meet housing costs in full for those on or below a certain level of income (e.g. the basic income recommended by the Commission on Social Welfare), regardless of its source, tapering off as incomes rise above this level. Such a benefit would provide assistance to employed people renting in the private sector who currently receive none, and would be more equitable. It would ease the problems of local authorities in recovering rent arrears.

Commitment to a comprehensive housing policy is political. Governments to date have shown little interest in the housing needs of the poor and marginalised members of our society. The need for a change in direction is clear. The challenge to those who believe in that need is to make it a political reality.

Reference
O'Brien, L., and Dillon, B., *Private Rented: the Forgotten Sector,* Threshold, 1982, Dublin.

CHAPTER 3

Housing policy as it affects Travelling people

*John Cauley/Michael Collins/Mervyn Ennis/
Thomas McCann/Chrissey Sullivan*

92.8% of families in 'serviced sites' lack a connector to
public electricity supplies and 99.4% are without hot
water tap, bath or shower facilities.

In a democratic society, men are not to be understood as the subjects of administrative rules, but such rules should facilitate the life of men in the community to which he belongs . . . (Liewen, 1969).

Introduction

We are all too well aware of our paper's limitations but this is the *first* time that we as Travellers have been consulted and encouraged to give an active voice, rather than getting settled people to act as brokers on our behalf, and we are grateful for this opportunity.

Prejudice

The greatest problem affecting Travelling people in Ireland is prejudice and not even the proposed Anti-Race Bill could get close to the very subtle forms of prejudice that face the Travellers, especially in the areas of housing, education and welfare. Most of the early reports on Travellers were openly prejudiced, but this was never challenged.

For example, the Commission on Itinerancy was set up in June 1960, with the following terms of reference:

1. to enquire into the problem arising from the presence in the country of itinerants in considerable numbers.
2. to examine the economic, educational, health and social problems inherent in their way of life.
3. to promote their absorption into the general community.

According to these terms of reference, 'itinerants' were a problem to the community. Their way of life was non-viable, unacceptable, and inherently riddled with problems. Indeed, there could be no final solution, until itinerant families were absorbed into the general community through housing (Commission on Itinerancy, 1963). Because the terms of reference were not clear the report was equally prejudiced. This Report and its recommendations became the corner-stone of Government policy and of the work of the Settlement Committee which tried to implement its recommendations on a pilot basis.

Aspirations of Travellers

Absorption into housing was to be the most frequent and urgently repeated recommendation of the Commission. However, this policy did not reflect the particular wishes, needs and aspirations of the Travelling people. Travellers wanted – then as now – proper parking grounds, legalised, approved and with proper facilities. These halting places would replace those traditional camping sites that were increasingly being taken over by both public and private developers (O'Donoghue, 1960).

It is a sad reflection on Dublin local authorities that today – twenty seven years later – this basic right remains a pipe dream for most Travellers in the Eastern Health Board region.

Travellers were seen as inadequate people – a motley collection of drop-outs from particular events in Irish history who became, in time, the tinkers of Ireland. Tinkers were synonymous with thieves, rogues, robbers, misfits, inadequates, who needed to be rehabilitated.

Rehabilitation of itinerants is still stated as the objective of the Department of the Environment – it is used as the reason for the employment of social workers and administrative people in the itinerant section of the local authorities.

Local authority policy on Travellers differs considerably from the Travellers' own policy which is based on their definition of themselves, as a separate ethnic group within Irish society, who have their own language, traditions and way of life which are different from those of the majority culture. In brief, the Government policy for twenty seven years has been totally negative regarding Travellers. It did not consult them on their needs. It viewed them as 'inadequates' in need of rehabilitation. Its policy was one of absorption which was recently watered down to integration and assimilation, but it means the same thing.

The differences between the Government policy of the 1960s as stated in the Report on the Commission on Itinerancy (1963) and the 1980s Review Body (The Travelling People Review Body, 1983) are merely cosmetic.

Sites, Services and Facilities

There has been a limited provision of serviced sites by Dublin Corporation and County Council. Generally, the locations are secluded from the settled population. The stated policy of Dublin Corporation on the provision of sites is that: sites must be within reach of services such as buses, shops, churches but at a convenient distance from the settled community.

Apart from discriminatory elements, it must be noted that this policy is at variance with the absorption policy. In practice the location of sites, has, by and large, been on wasteland. See the map (Appendix 3.1) for example: Labre Park – the first site for Travellers – is a wasteland along the canal at Ballyfermot. Due to the size and amount of electrical pylons in the area, this land could not be used for anything, and housing for the settled community would never be allowed there.

Avila Park was sited on the offcut for a proposed new north road; Dunsink site is next to the toxic waste dump; Clondalkin is next to the new prison, and the site located on a wet field, unsuitable for building purposes.

The vast majority of locations were unsuitable for any commercial or housing purposes so they were suitable for Travellers. The actual provision of tigeens on serviced sites leaves a lot to be desired, for example those at Avila, Labre and Cara, were intended as temporary structures.

The term 'serviced sites' is a misnomer because of the families resident in serviced sites, 22.3% have no piped water supply, 37.6% lack toilet facilities, 99.4% are without a hot water tap and the same percentage without bath/shower facilities; 92.8% lack a connector to public electricity supplies (Rottman and others, 1986, p.53).

Mincéir Mislí rally at the General Post Office, Dublin, July 1984

Travellers Have no Rights

The attitude of local authorities to its tenants is generally accepted as being a landlord and tenant relationship. As Travellers are seen as inadequate tenants, we have no rights. Consequently, local authorities have been able to shift and shunt us about, from place to place.

We are no one's responsibility. "The circumstances of the Irish Travelling people are intolerable. No humane and decent society, once made aware of such circumstances, could permit them to persist" (Rottman and others, 1986, p.73). The vast majority of people who work for Travellers are local authority employees, funded by local authorities, and their criticism of the organisation is very rare and not tolerated.

There is no voice active on behalf of Travellers. No county has provided for the projected growth of Traveller numbers predicted for their area in 1960 (Commission on Itinerancy, 1963). \

A report published by the Conference of Major Religious Superiors, 1986, estimated from a study of population growth among Travellers that 275 houses a year, together with thirty five sites of ten caravans per year for the next five years *is the minimum* start required to meet the Travellers' need for accommodation. At £30,000 per house and £250,000 per equipped site, it is envisaged that an

expenditure of some £17 million per year is required.

The stark reality of our position is that we believe this amount of money will not be made available to cope with our desperate situation. The political, moral, ethical or religious will does not exist to give Travellers their rights. To bring about change and to try to gain our rights through Court proceedings is far too expensive and beyond our capacity as Travellers at present. We are small in number, poorly organised and have no power, money or political influence to affect policy. The future for us Travelling People looks bleak indeed.

We believe that the vast majority of people, particularly in the Dublin area, who are employed to work *for* Travelling people are merely a smoke-screen, to camouflage the reality and make small gains in our favour.

Social workers, administrators, site attendants, home-makers, nurses and the whole caring merry-go-round can only continue to treat the symptoms. This is as long as the underlying prejudice remains unchallenged and the Travellers are left with no place to make home, and no power to change things.

Recommendations

We recommend that:

1. Travellers continue to be encouraged to become involved in self-help projects.
2. An immediate plan of action be undertaken to provide basic human living conditions for Travellers.
3. The inter-agency political rivalry between local authorities dealing with Travellers be discontinued. For example, Dublin Corporation and Dublin County Council disagreement over the provision of sites. (Dublin Corporation has only two sites altogether catering for twenty five families within Dublin city boundaries.)
4. Local authorities pay immediate attention to providing water, sanitation, accommodation, medical care.
5. Local authorities stop treating Travellers as a problem group and stop taking an annual head count of Travellers, locally and nationally.
6. Travelling people themselves be enabled to carry out proper research on their own history, traditions and culture.
7. Legal aid be provided to help Travellers bring to court local authorities which are neglectful of their responsibilities to Travellers.
8. Legal aid be provided to help tackle the wider patterns of discrimination in Irish society.

References

Report on the Commission on Itinerancy, Stationery Office, 1963, Dublin.

Rottman, David B., Tussing, A. Dale and Wiley, Miriam M., *The Population Structure and Living Circumstances of Irish Travellers: Results from the 1981 Census of Traveller Families,* Paper No. 131, The Economic and Social Research Institute, 1986, Dublin.

The Travelling People Review Body, *Report,* Stationery Office, 1983, Dublin.

Appendix 3.1 Traveller Sites in Dublin

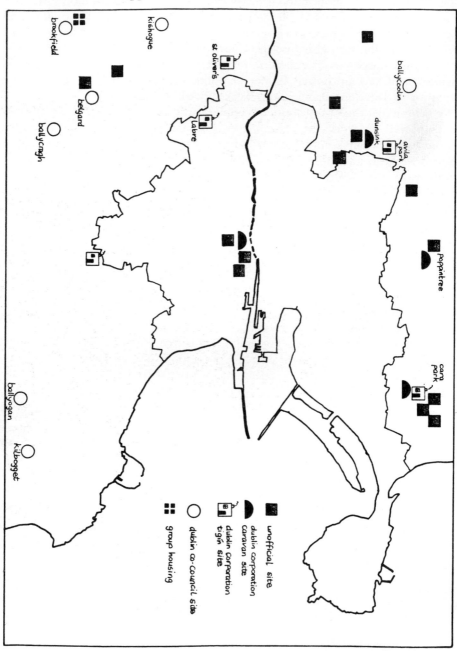

Belcamp Site, North Dublin.

CHAPTER 4

Youth homelessness

Justin O'Brien

Young homeless people are not a very identifiable group. They appear the same as any other young people during the day.

It is very frightening when you are young. You are vulnerable to drugs and prostitution. You have no money and it's very hard to get any when you are not at the age of getting money, because you have no address. You can't get any work because you have to be clean and tidy. You have to shoplift for food because you get into trouble with the police for dossing around. You can't go to any of your friends because they can't afford to keep you and they have no room.

      – A young person's description of being homeless.

Introduction

The closure of Hope Hostel in Dublin for homeless boys in April 1986 because of the lack of adequate funding being provided by the Eastern Health Board provoked considerable controversy and media coverage. It focussed attention on the needs of young people who were homeless and evoked interest and concern from the public. People rightly asked how it can be, in 1986, that young people are sleeping out at night, away from their homes and the State cannot respond? The answer to that question raises many further questions and issues. Under our existing child care legislation – the 1908 Children's Act – the State *via* the Health Boards are responsible for providing care and protection for children and young persons up to the age of sixteen years.

For young people between the ages of sixteen and eighteen years, there is no State agency responsible for their care and protection. If young people decide to leave home, or are forced to do so, they are faced with major difficulties. As they are not adults, they have no statutory entitlement to public housing. Their application would not even be considered. They may receive some financial assistance under the Supplementary Allowance Scheme. However, as this scheme is discretionary, the granting of financial aid is variable. Even if a young person has a source of income, they often find it difficult to acquire private rented accommodation because of their age. Thus, if young people find themselves out of home they are quickly caught in a cycle of homelessness with no address, no food, no income, no supportive relationships. This is as the young person described it at the beginning of this chapter.

Why Young People Become Homeless

Focus Point identified three factors which create homelessness among young people. The first factor is primarily one of poor family relationships, where there is poor communication between the young person and his/her parents over behaviour, attitudes, or where there are issues of conflict – such as violence, sexual or drug abuse, pregnancy, delinquency, unemployment. These issues may cause the young person to leave home or to be rejected by parents.

The second factor is where young people migrate to Dublin or any other city in search of employment, or wish to live independently of his/her family. This is a normal process in our society. The majority of people make this transition successfully – but a minority do not. Their search for employment fails. Their income is inadequate and they do not have secure accommodation. They can easily find themselves going between friends and acquaintances, or entering a hostel. Because of this process of displacement, their ties with their families weaken and they can easily fall into a cycle of homelessness and disaffiliation.

The third factor is that of young people leaving residential child care homes. These young people have been placed in care at an early age. Their ties and attachments to their natural family are limited or non-existent. They have no secure family to rely on if their education/employment/accommodation fails. If they leave care between the ages of sixteen and eighteen years the State has no more responsibility to provide financial aid, accommodation or protection for them.

How Many Young People Out-of-Home?

There are no accurate figures as to the number of young homeless people in Ireland. A survey by the National Campaign for the Homeless (1985) identified 390 persons under twenty years who were homeless in Ireland. A report by a group of social workers and members of voluntary organisations established that there were 328 (244 males and 84 females) young people under twenty five years who were homeless in Dublin in 1986 (Report by a Group of Social Workers and members of voluntary organisations 1986).

Focus Point indicates from its research and services that the young homeless population is a large one. From September 1985 to September 1986, 252 (29%) of persons who used the Focus Point Advice and Information and Telephone Services, were young people under twenty years of age. Of this 252, there were 147 males and 105 females, four were young people under twelve years of age, eighty four were between twelve and sixteen years, and 164 were between sixteen and twenty years. Focus Point Outreach Service – which makes contact with young unattached homeless people on the streets – met another 211 persons under twenty years in this same period. Of these, thirteen were under fourteen years, twenty were under sixteen years, and 178 were aged between sixteen and twenty years. The Outreach Service concentrates its work mainly in the inner city and therefore does not include young people living rough outside that area. What is striking from Focus Point's statistics is that youth homelessness is not primarily a male problem. Over 40% of those under twenty years who used Focus Point services were young women (Focus Point, 1986).

Research from the hostels indicate a similar pattern (Focus Point survey, 1986). On the census survey night of February 8th 1986, the bed occupancy rate was 112 males and 57 females: a total of 169 people under twenty years of age. These bed places include emergency, short-term and long-term hostels.

During the month of February 1986, there was a high rate of mobility amongst young people in and out of emergency and short-term hostels. In the boys' emergency and short term hostels there were thirty one new arrivals and thirty nine departures. In the girls' emergency hostels, there were fifteen new arrivals and

If young people find themselves out of home, they are quickly caught in a cycle of homelessness, with no address, no food, no income, no supportive relationships.

twelve departures. This gives a total of forty six new arrivals and fifty one departures over a four-week period.

Services

Given the dimensions of youth homelessness, one could reasonably expect a committed response and a range of services available from the State agencies. Sadly, young people are not a priority with the Eastern Health Board Community Care services. As stated, there are no services provided for those over sixteen years of age. Social work intervention which could address family difficulties and provide support for young persons in their families is not available at present. For those between the ages of fourteen and sixteen years, there is a very limited service provision at community level and residential levels. There are only two youth projects run by the Eastern Health Board in Dublin and there has been a reduction in the number of residential places for older children and young adolescents (Department of Health, 1983; Burke, Carney and Cook, 1981). It is extremely difficult for a social worker to find any residential placements for young people. This was aptly or grimly illustrated in 1986 when no suitable residential or alternative placement for a young homeless boy of thirteen could be found. This resulted in him being placed in a high security unit which was recognised as being unsuitable for the boy (*The Irish Press*, 23 July 1986).

Fostering placements are usually not available for older children, and professional fostering care has not been developed by the Eastern Health Board. Of the existing hostels for young people in Dublin, there are different levels of funding provided by the state agencies and many are inadequately funded and poorly resourced. If a young homeless person commits an offence, support is more likely to be more readily available from the Juvenile Liaison Service or Social Work Service of the Welfare Section of the Department of Justice.

The provision of care and support for young homeless people has been in the main provided by the voluntary sector. Youth work services are primarily provided by voluntary groups. In recent years, however, Comhairle le Leas Óige has developed its services by employing youth workers to work in local communities with unattached people and also provides funding to some voluntary bodies working with young homeless people. While this has been a major improvement, it is still not a comprehensive youth work service.

Young People Who Have Been in Care

Young people who have been in care form a significant number of the young homeless population. Children are received into care because their families are unable to care and provide for them, and the State undertakes that responsibility. Research here and in the United States indicated clearly that children who are received into care are a very disadvantaged group (Tizard *et al* 1975; Payne *et al*, 1979; Holman, 1980; Richardson, 1985).

John, a young person of seventeen years, who has availed of Focus Point services, has written about himself:

49

I was put into care at six years of age because my mother had problems with my father. I was put into a home in Dublin. I stayed there for three years. I was going home for weekends in that period of time. The nuns at the home felt I was getting too wild, so they moved me to another home for three months, and then another nearby. My social worker felt I should go to another home, because the one I was in was not a short term home. I was there for four years. After doing my Group Cert, my time was up in care. So, I left to go home. I was looking forward to this – and when I got home everyone was glad to see me.

I was home for a month, getting on well and looking for a job. But after a while things started to get rough. The children were blaming me on things I did not do. My mother was jumping down my throat.

Then John left home. He has been homeless for the past year. Since he was received into the care of the State at the age of six years, he was reared in four different children's homes. Since he left care, he has lived in five different hostels. Most of these were hostels for adult men and not suitable for his particular needs. Sometimes John chose to leave these hostels. Other times he had to leave because of mistakes he made. To date, his life has been one of change and insecurity. Other people have always made decisions for and about him. The State which took responsibility to rear him at the age of six is now no longer responsible as John is over sixteen years of age.

Focus Point's experience is that young people who have been in care form a significant group of the homeless population. Of the 211 persons which the Outreach service of Focus Point met, some sixty three had been in care. This pattern is not unique in Ireland. A study of single homeless adults in England found that 13% of respondents of all ages had been in care at some stage in their lives (Department of the Environment, 1981). A review of 1,000 young people in Glasgow by the District Council's Homeless Persons Unit showed that 13% of all appicants had come straight from care (Shelter, Scotland, 1984).

Other research shows that young people who have been in care have little or no experience of being in control of events in their lives. Admission to care has been sudden and traumatic. They have little understanding of events or involvement in the plans that are made for them (Morgan-Klein, 1985). They are then expected to live independently, manage a home, secure employment or live with unemployment. It is an indictment of the State that it cannot provide adequate resources and supports to the residential homes to enable them to provide an aftercare service.

In 1969 the Kennedy Report recommended that ". . . every Residential Home and Special School should have an aftercare agent who should co-ordinate the work of paving the way for a child's release" and that "Before a child is discharged from Residential Care it must be ensured that he will have suitable accommodation" (Kennedy, 1969). Some eighteen years later, these recommendations have not been implemented.

Being Young and Homeless

The young homeless population are a very mobile group, moving between hostels, sleeping rough, dossing with friends, moving back home for temporary periods.

They tend not to avail of structured services, and often find the existing community care, youth work and training workshops either unsuitable or inaccessible. They also tend not to use the formal social service networks sometimes out of feelings of fear or because they do not identify with these structures, or simply because they have no knowledge of their existence. Young homeless people are not a very visible or identifiable group of people. They appear the same as any other young person during the day. At nightime, however, this group becomes vulnerable to the raw exploitation of street life. It is not unusual for them to become involved in crime, male and female prostitution, alcohol and drug abuse. A young person describes his situation:

It's like you are going around with blokes who're sleeping out rough like yourself, right? And they're into drugs, maybe that's why they left home in the first place, their parents couldn't accept they were taking drugs. When you're in the gang you are tempted to take stuff cause you want to stay with them.

Another young person, Cathy, who had been in care for five and a half years wrote about her situation living in a hostel:

I found that living in a hostel they don't prepare you to live independently . . . they don't help you with cooking and budgeting and what to look for when you are looking for a flat. A typical day at the hostel was like this. We got up when we were called at 8.00 a.m. Then we went to work. When we came home the dinner was on the table at 6.00 p.m. All the shopping was done for us and all the bills were paid. We just gave in our rent every week, £15.00, but we never knew about the cost of living, because everything was done for us. From the hostel I went to live in an interim housing project.

I think there is a definite need for this type of accommodation. I was helped in this house to cook and budget my money. I had my own freedom and I looked after myself in general. After living there I went to live in a private flat – the landlady wasn't registered. I left there as I couldn't afford the rent and I went to stay with friends and sometimes I'd stay in hostels. Then after a while, I went to look for a Corporation place. I eventually got a flat and when I moved I had nothing.

This is my experience of coping alone and I was one of the lucky ones. The reason why I was one of the lucky ones was that I found a job, I had income and I had the support of the Focus Point staff. I also had friends and sisters living in the area where I got my Corporation flat.

Conclusions

The failure of the State to address of the young homeless represents its failure to give priority to socially disadvantaged children and young people.

Successive Governments have appointed various commissions and committees which over the past twenty years have recommended changes in policies and structure of services for children and young people. These include the Commission on Reformatory and Industrial Schools (Kennedy, 1969), the Task Force (1980) and the National Youth Policy Committee (1984) – the latter referred very specifically to the needs of young homeless people. They recommended that legislation be enacted to place a statutory responsibility on some public authority for making provision for homeless young people, that services be developed to help them, and that income support be provided for them. These recommendations have not been implemented. Our children's legislation and services remain unreformed some twenty years after the first Government committee was appointed.

The legislative reforms needed should clearly define the role and responsibility of the State and its agencies. First, it should be the clear duty and responsibility of the Department of Health and the Health Boards to provide care and protection for children and young people up to the age of eighteen years.

Second, it should be the responsibility of the local authority to provide housing for young people. Guidelines should be established which would give priority to young people leaving residential care and to 16-18 year olds who become homeless.

Third, a range of non-residential services should be provided which include the following:

1. The extension and development of community services, i.e., family support services, youth work services, intermediate treatment which would prevent young people becoming homeless and would provide support for them when they return home;

2. The provision of a range of hostel accommodation – emergency, short-term and long-term – for young people who cannot live at home;

3. The development of specialised residential care and foster care for young people and children who have special needs and difficulties;

4. The development and extension of Outreach services, day activities, advice and information, training and settlement services for young people who are currently homeless;

5. The provision of supportive accommodation, such as interim housing, independent living units, shared accommodation for young people who cannot live alone or independently.

Finally, it has to be recognised that no one agency would be able or likely to provide the above. A council should be established involving representatives of the Health Board, Local Authority, Department of Justice, Local Youth Service Board and representatives of appropriate voluntary bodies involved which would be responsible for the planning and provision of the above services.

52

References

Burke, H., Carney, C., Cook, G., Editors, *Youth and Justice — Young Offenders in Ireland*, Turoe Press, 1981, Dublin.

Commission on Reformatory and Industrial Schools (Kennedy), *Report*, Stationery Office, 1969, Dublin.

Department of the Environment, *Single and Homeless*, H.M.S.O., 1981, London.

Department of Health, *Children in Care*, Stationery Office, 1983, Dublin.

Focus Point, *The Extent and Nature of Homelessness in Dublin*, Focus Point Unpublished Survey, 1986, Dublin.

Focus Point, *The Present and Preferred Accommodation of Young Unemployed People in Dublin*, Unpublished Survey, 1986, Dublin.

Holman, R., *Inequality in Child Care*, Child Poverty Action Group, 1980, London.

Irish Press, 23 July, 1986, Dublin.

Kennedy, Kennedy Report 1969.

Morgan-Klein, B., *A Report on Young People Leaving Care in Scotland*, Scottish Council for the Single Homeless, 1985, Edinburgh.

National Campaign for the Homeless, Ireland's Young Homeless, 1985, Dublin.

National Youth Policy Committee, *Final Report*, Stationery Office, 1984, Dublin.

Payne, C., White, K., *Caring for Deprived Children*, Croom Helm, 1979, London.

Report on the Reformatory and Industrial Schools System, Stationery Office, 1969, Dublin.

Richardson, V., *Whose Children?* U.C.D. Family Studies Unit, 1985, Dublin.

Report by a Group of Social Workers and Members of Voluntary Organisations, *Care and Accommodation for Young People at Risk or Homeless in Dublin*, 1986, Dublin.

Shelter Scotland, 1984.

Task Force, *Task Force on Child Care Services and Final Report*, Stationery Office, 1980, Dublin.

Tizard, J., Sinclair I., Clarke, R.G., *Varieties of Residential Experience*, Kegan Paul, 1975, London.

CHAPTER 5

Ballymun: Twenty one years on

John Sweeney

Amenities are inadequate in Ballymun. The above is a local shop.

Introduction

The housing policy designed by planners and officials has up to now been based largely on physical considerations: numbers of houses needed, size and quality of buildings and the price of land. It has rarely taken into account the way in which communities will actually live out their daily lives. Although great strides have been made in providing shelter for people in need of houses in the Dublin area, the effects of housing policies which are concerned mainly with the provision of housing and not with the provision of facilities and the daily living requirements of people, are being felt by the communities who have to live in the estates and tower blocks hurriedly constructed by a Corporation faced with a housing problem.

Background

In 1966, the first tenants moved into Ireland's largest, high-rise estate. For three years they continued to be surrounded by construction activity as the rest of the 2,814 flats and 400 houses were finished around them. The space-age architecture of the estate, the use of a building system totally new to Ireland, the sheer scale of the development, the spaciousness of the flats and houses, spoke eloquently of the 1960s.

Politicians and technocrats who could conceive, plan and carry out such rapid provision of accommodation would certainly be capable of implementing their promises of promoting a balanced development where different types of families would share the amenities and facilities proper to a town of 16,000 people.

Since its completion in 1969, the Ballymun estate has been extended and a further 1,495 houses added so that, today, it comprises some 4,709 homes for approximately 20,000 people. It has never enjoyed a balanced population mix though a single authority, Dublin Corporation, controls virtually all movement into the estate. Its one supermarket and two pubs are patent examples of its inadequate facilities: derelict vans and stranded containers house small shops that are the only expansion undertaken by commercial interests there since 1969.

As the Irish economy has slipped from the 'best of decades' when economic growth was rapid and emigration ceased, to the chronic unemployment of the 1980s, the population in Ballymun seems to have been pushed right off the ladder. Unemployment on the estate was two and half per centage points higher than Strabane in Northern Ireland at the end of 1985, a population centre of comparable size and regarded as the North's unemployment black spot (Ballymun Community Coalition, 1986). Poverty is familiar and would be on the scale of an epidemic if Community Welfare Officers were not disbursing some one million pounds a year in the area and the Society of St Vincent de Paul over £200,000. The dream is developing a horror ending. The big-thinking and self-confidence of the politicians and technocrats of the 1960s has been replaced by a defensiveness and deepening worry in their colleagues of the 1980s. Has Ballymun a future?

What Has Gone Wrong?

Ballymun was thought up as a response to a new type of homelessness that emerged with chilling suddenness in 1963. In June that year, four people died in Dublin when, first, no. 20 Bolton Street and, then, nos. 3 and 4 Fenian Street collapsed without warning. Dublin awoke to the horror of dangerous buildings. Within a fortnight of the Bolton Street tragedy, the Corporation had to handle 1,500 emergency calls from people concerned about the safety of their homes.

There followed a spate of Dangerous Buildings Notices and people being displaced from such houses were given immediate priority in new allocations by the Corporation. Within six months (i.e. by January, 1964), 837 dwellings had been allocated to people displaced from dangerous buildings.

Reading through the *Reports and Printed Documents of the Corporation of Dublin,* (Corporation of Dublin, 1964), it is notable how little the Corporation panicked. It defended its record and pointed to a full programme of flat and house construction. Nearly all the flats were being built in the city centre where, the Corporation claimed, the demand for flats was. On the perimeter, it was just about to begin building 1,100 houses in Coolock. It was doing all it could with its existing technical and other staffs. When the Dáil came back from its summer recess and debated the new housing crisis in Dublin in October, it began to become apparent that the then Minister for Local Government was not convinced that the Corporation's all was going to be enough. Mr Neil Blaney began to coax the Corporation to consider something big and something new.

There was always something of a prestige nature in what was to become the Ballymun project. A dialogue took place during 1964 and 1965 between the Minister for Local Government and Dublin Corporation that centred around buildings methods.

Industrialised or system building had not been attempted in Ireland before and seemed to be worth pursuing in an economy whose rapid expansion was already giving rise to bottlenecks in the supply of skilled labour, and industrialised building economised on skilled labour. In late 1964 and early 1965, the Minister set out to convince the City Council that it should invite his Department to plan and have constructed a major, new system-built scheme. Four of his advisors took seventeen Councillors and Corporation officials on a week long tour of inspection of system-built estates on the Continent in April, 1964. They came back suitably impressed at the *technical* achievements they had seen. They reported that new system-building could provide a large number of new dwellings without disturbing Dublin Corporation's set housing programme, i.e. without pulling existing technical and other skilled Corporation staff away from other work. Subsequently, there was detailed discussion between the Minister and the Corporation on the specifics of the heating of this housing scheme.

There was a total lack of comment at this time on the *social* implications of high-rise developments, save for this clanger: "It was apparent also from the schemes investigated that suburban housing by way of multi-storey flats has provided a *seemingly satisfactory form of community development* in the cities visited" (Corporation of Dublin, 1964, No. 62, emphasis added). Nothing about the social dangers that such developments were even then posing in other countries. Nothing about the matching policies on tenanting, maintenance and facilities that were the conditions necessary for turning a technical accomplishment into a social one. Perhaps one could expect nothing more profound from a delegation of twenty one who visited three cities in three countries in one week. Perhaps it was part of the 1960s to give technical solutions to human problems.

Whatever the root cause, Dublin Corporation found itself, in 1969, the landlord of a high-rise complex to which Central Government had conceived and given birth. The mechanics of building it had enabled the Corporation to continue its own building programme without hindrance. The challenge of tenanting and maintaining the scheme, however, was to need resources that the Corporation simply did not have, resources of imagination, finance and power. Imaginative policies on tenanting were called for to avoid an unbalanced population structure developing. Additional finance needed to be available to the Corporation's maintenance section to prevent competition from other and newer areas slowly eroding the high standards that such a flat complex needs. A co-ordinated approach to the broader development of the area needed to be demanded from the private sector and the relevant State bodies. On these three fronts, however, the Corporation was hopelessly ill-prepared.

As early as 1965 the need for non-commercial community facilities was acknowledged, principally a library, health clinic, halls, swimming pool and gymnasium.

The provision of these by the relevant authorities was seen as improving the environment for further commercial developments by the private sector, and a skating rink, cinema and dance hall were all talked of. The twenty one years since the building of the estate, however, show a patchy record by the relevant public bodies and a dismal performance by the private sector, which has reacted harshly to the erosion of purchasing power in the area. A swimming pool was built only under extreme pressure from tenants, a good public library was provided, a health clinic was built, which subsequently turned out to be too small, and only now are some small community halls being built.

In the private sector, Quinnsworth took over the Five Star supermarket chain in 1979 and subsequently closed down one of the two supermarkets in Ballymun, so as not to be in competition with itself. The Bank of Ireland pulled out in 1983, leaving the area dependent on one Allied Irish Bank branch. Standards of maintenance in what was once one of Dublin's newest shopping centres have dropped, and the leases on the units have experienced an increasingly rapid turnover.

Ballymun in the 1970s: Housing the Very Young

For most of the past twenty one years Ballymun received young families so that it was children and young parents who found their social needs uncatered for and the standard of maintenance of their homes slipping.

58

A survey in 1974 found that 40% of its population was aged ten or under and about 25% was between twenty one and thirty (Ballymun Amenities Group, 1974). The difficulties of bringing up young children in high-rise flats dominate the findings of this Report.

The average family in the fifteen storey blocks had two children under six. This was remarkable evidence of a mismatch between what was intended and what happened. On 8 January 1965, when Mr Blaney outlined his Department's plans for Ballymun to the Corporation, it was explicitly stated that the fifteen storeys "would provide especially for small adult households of one, two and three persons". This, I believe, is one of the chief factors behind the myth that Ballymun proves that "Irish people don't take to living in flats". Irish people, in fact, are willing to pay good money for 'apartments', as some property developers have discovered to their advantage, (a flat becomes an 'apartment', it seems, if it is in a private complex and maintained to a high standard!) But the Irish people in question do not, as a rule, have young children. It is probable that in few European countries, if any, do parents take easily to rearing young children in high-rise flats. But this is overwhelmingly what Ballymun was used for in its first fifteen years.

The 1974 report commented fairly: "nobody thought very seriously about the people who were going to live in Ballymun. If they did, they simply assumed that the families would not all have young children, and that there would certainly be no need to put those families in the tower-blocks."

As early as 1972, a small survey showed that a supervised playground and a nursery were easily the most missed facilities in the area (Croskery, 1972). A 1975 study noted that only eight play groups existed although a minimum of twenty five were reckoned to be needed, and that a total population of 15,000 had only eight relatively small adult clubs (Muldowney and Mulhall, 1975). Local people subsequently worked to provide what prior planning had made no provision for, and developed a strong network of pre-school, community play groups.

However, the fact remains that young parents with children in Ballymun have always had difficulty in getting the vital supports they need from the wider community – such as supervised play areas, creche facilities, an agreeable environment and social and cultural meeting places.

For these reasons – no follow-through on the promises that Ballymun would have a full range of amenities, and the unsuitability of high-rise accommodation for families with young children – an outflow from the estate began, from as early as 1972.

The 1972 survey reckoned that 56% did not intend to stay and that 29% were on the housing transfer list. The 1974 report, based on a larger survey, estimated that about 25% were waiting for houses and noted that people were not staying long; of all tenants in the estate in March 1974, only half had been there in January 1971. The evidence seems clear that, at this early stage, the Corporation began to use parts of Ballymun as a half-way house, somewhere to send young families for a number of years until either more children brought their points up to the necessary level for entitlement to a house, or the Corporation's house building programme caught up with the demand and married couples with three or fewer children could be given a house.

Ballymun: Housing the Residual

It is this last development which has struck Ballymun with the force of a storm in the 1980s. Families that had been 'stored' in the Ballymun flats for years were, at last, offered houses in the early 1980s as new estates in Tallaght, Clondalkin and Blanchardstown were built.

This outflow was accentuated by the introduction of the £5,000 grant by the Department of the Environment to local authority tenants who would buy a house in the private sector. Suddenly, the Corporation found itself facing a situation for which it was quite unprepared – a surfeit of flats. Over 400 are now empty. Its provision for making temporary empty flats secure have been exhausted and a growing number are vandalised. It has relaxed its procedures for making squatters into legal tenants. These developments are making matters worse for the tenants who remain. Of most interest, however, are recent trends in the type of person which the Corporation is now sending to the estate. Here, I shall draw heavily on a recent study done by a community group, which is the most comprehensive I know of its type in the area.

This study, *A Block of Facts* confirms what people living in the area had suspected was happening (SUSS Community Group, 1987). In the first place, 1985 witnessed a huge increase of 124% in the total number of new lettings in Ballymun. Over five years 1980-1984, the total number of new lettings in the estate declined from a high of 887 in 1980 to 650 in 1984.

They jumped from 650 to 1,459 in 1985, evidence of an unwelcome increase in transience which continued into 1986 and which has reversed the pattern of slow improvement. Reading the full report, it becomes clear that what is now happening is that married couples with children are being moved out of the flats and single-parent families and single people are being moved in.

This has happened in two stages. Between 1980 and 1984, the number of married couples being given accommodation in Ballymun dropped by over one half but the number of single parents getting accommodation nearly doubled. Nineteen eighty four was the first year in which, of people being given new lettings in Ballymun, the number of single women was greater than the number of married couples.

The impact of this in city-wide terms is considerable. For example, in the twelve month period to the end of September 1985 the Ballymun flats gave accommodation to 45% of all the single parents housed by the Corporation, although it accounts for only some 10% of Dublin Corporation stock of dwellings. This first stage took place, as was already mentioned, in the context of a steady decline in the overall level of transience in the area.

The second stage occurred in 1985 and 1986: while there was no diminution in the number of single women getting accommodation, there was a huge surge in the number of single men. The average number of new lettings being given to single men was less than twenty a year in the five years 1980-1984.

In 1985 alone, 231 such lettings were given, nearly two and a half times the total for the preceding five years, and in the first seven months of 1986, the number was 242 or 33% of all new lettings in that period.

A further challenging finding of the SUSS report is that this newer category of householder is more than likely to be given what is regarded, even within Ballymun, as the least popular type of flat – accommodation in the eight-storey blocks.

The implications of all this are grave. It might seem that, to some extent, what is now happening is close to what was intended by the planners in 1965; for example, that the fifteen-storey blocks would be primarily for small adult households. It must be immediately pointed out, however, that 'small, adult households' also describes the occupants of private apartments in Dublin's southside. There is no evidence that the planners had in mind households on exceptionally low incomes and labouring under specific social disadvantages, though that is what is happening.

No Consultation

Housing policy – in Dublin at least – seems to require the existence of one or a few 'neglectable' areas. In the words of the SUSS report:

> The large number of single people now being given accommodation in Ballymun is not an accident. It is not something which no-one could forsee. There is a single controlling authority handling all allocations to the estate. It is astonishing that such a dramatic innovation in Dublin Corporation's housing policy should have been unannounced and never debated by the City Council. It has never been acknowledged by the Corporation nor explained to residents of the area. It has only become apparent after the event. This raises questions. When, how, and by whom, was the decision made?
>
> Who will own responsibility for the policy now in force and discuss its implications with residents in the area, the schools, professional community and social workers, etc? If there are to be further dramatic changes in Corporation policy towards the area, will there be a similar absence of consultation with those whose lives and work are seriously affected by changes in the social mix of the population?

The SUSS report necessarily and effectively takes the standpoint of a local community, and argues a point of basic justice. It is also, surely, not in the interests of Dublin at large that one housing estate should be used as a type of open area, a place to give accommodation to a disproportionate share of the city's low-income and socially disadvantaged householders. Such a policy breeds ghettos of two sorts, high-income and low-income, and fosters prejudice and stereotyping throughout the community.

Economic Deprivation

The SUSS report 1987 stated:

The implications of what has been happening for the already high level of economic hardship in the area has become only too apparent to community workers, voluntary and statutory alike. Single parents and single people eligible for local authority accommodation tend to have low incomes.

Circumstantial evidence abounds that the number of people needing financial assistance from community welfare officers, the Society of St Vincent de Paul and the local parishes has increased.

The evidence is now more than circumstantial, as the following returns for Ballymun in 1985 by the Community Welfare section of the Eastern Health Board indicate:

	£
Total supplementary welfare expenditure	997,706
Current fuel scheme expenditure	145,940
Current footwear scheme expenditure	38,419
Total number of supplementary welfare allowance payments	26,444
Average weekly caseload per Community Welfare Officer	101

It can be seen that the health board alone supplemented the incomes of families and individuals in Ballymun with £1.182m. in 1985. Those with experience of the administration of supplementary welfare will know that this figure measures real hardship and desperation. It reflects the large number of new arrivals to the estates who have practically no household resources. It points to the struggle of single parents and long-term unemployed people with ESB bills, back-to-school expenses, money lenders and the like.

These figures alone should expose the folly of continuing to send people who are economically impoverished to an area already so over burdened.

No Amenities

A third observation made by the SUSS group:

As they stand, social amenities are quite inadequate for the new tenants of Ballymun. Where for example, can a single parent go to meet people socially if there is nowhere to leave children? In an area now home to so many single people, what social amenities are there to enjoy? An interesting comparison can be made with the Ranelagh/Rathmines area of the city which also houses a large number of single people. It has restaurants, cafes, health clubs, launderettes, etc., far in excess of those in Ballymun. It seems that, more than ever, the need for facilities in Ballymun outstrips the willingness of the public or private sectors to provide them.

Ballymun was thought up as a response to a new type of homelessness that emerged with chilling suddenness in 1963.

Those with the interests of the homeless at heart will know that it is no kindness to group them in an area where basic amenities are inadequate and where caring services are already under severe pressure.

Community Spirit and the Way Forward

The SUSS report was produced by a community group in Ballymun, people who – in difficult circumstances – designed and set up a service to their own area rather than resign themselves to unemployment. Ballymun has never lacked such groups and today boasts many.

The unique nature of the estate has consistently evoked a strong sense of identity and commitment to the area in many of its tenants. The SUSS report estimates that 42.5% of them intend staying permanently.

This is worth quoting given that the estate is known throughout Dublin as a form of transit camp. This substantial number of people form the foundation on which a better future can be built.

A small start has been made by the Corporation which now practises a limited form of consultation with tenants in one part of the estate on allocations policy. This pilot project (initiated in 1982 and which came into effect in 1984) though working well, has had no timetable put on it for evaluation and eventual extension to the rest of the estate. Much greater resources of imagination, finance and power will have to be available to the Corporation, however, if such collaboration is to show real results. In many ways, the Corporation should cease to be apologetic about Ireland's largest high-rise estate and actively market its flats which are solid, centrally heated, with hot water supplied, spacious, on the edge of open countryside and within four miles of the city centre. This could only happen, however, within the context of considerably improved standards of maintenance. So we are back to money. Yet the alternative, ironically, will be not less expenditure but more, under different headings and by different State bodies.

Instead of an increased maintenance budget there will be increased bills for vandalism, policing, health and even one day partial demolition which would be a real policy of despair. It would be nice if Neil Blaney would one day want restored the road-sign on the dual carriageway to Ballymun which commemorated his role in having it built.

References

Ballymun Amenities Group, *Ballymun: The Experiment that Failed*, 1974, Dublin.
Ballymun Community Coalition, *Ballymun: Its Future Can Work*, 1986, Dublin.
Corporation of Dublin, *Reports and Printed Documents*, City Hall Library, 1974, Dublin.
Croskery, Eithne, *Ballymun: A Survey of a Modern Housing Estate, its People and its Problems*, BA Dissertation, U.C.D., 1972, Dublin.
SUSS Community Group, *A Block of Facts: Ballymun, Twenty One Years On*, 1987, Dublin.

CHAPTER 6

Change through struggle: the North Inner City

Michael Rafferty

May 1979: Tenants from Gardiner Street, Sean McDermott Street, Summerhill and Gloucester Place stage a road-block over Dublin Corporation's neglect of their housing.

Introduction

The type of housing that can be seen dotted around the north inner city of Dublin was not regrettably the result of rational planning but of struggle and street protest. In this system, ask and you will be ignored, fight and it shall be given.

Apart from the tragedies at Bolton Street and Fenian Street in the early 1960s and the subsequent need to rehouse people living in dangerous buildings, there were other factors behind the grim housing conditions and shortages which were characteristics of the 1960s. One was the rapid upswing in the economy, which led to migration from the rural areas into a growing industrial capital city and a halt to emigration to Britain and America. Another was the extraordinary property boom characterised by arbitrary demolition of habitable houses by property speculators. Rent in private dwellings soared, resulting in overcrowding. Many homeless people squatted in Corporation property, with nearly 400 families doing this in 1970.

The DHAC

Out of this situation developed the Dublin Housing Action Committee (DHAC), which was to bring about the changes in policy whose fruits we see around us in the newly-built small schemes of Corporation houses dotted all over the north inner city area.

The DHAC analysed the cause of the 1960s housing shortage to be a mixture of property speculation and Government indifference. The campaign, which involved pickets, public meetings, riots with the police and direct action such as people chaining themselves to public buildings and interrupting meetings of Dublin City Council, reached its peak when Denis Dennehy was brought before the High Court for failing to vacate a flat in 20 Mountjoy Square on 3 January 1969. He was committed to Mountjoy jail and immediately went on hunger strike. After a series of protests, the DHAC organised the famous O'Connell Street sit-down on 18 January 1969.

The Garda reaction was to beat the homeless off the street. Michael Sweetman said at the time: "It seems to me that Dennehy is in prison precisely because being homeless he took shelter as a necessity. This may be strictly illegal but it is not immoral" (*Sunday Press*, 19 January 1969).

DHAC brought the housing issue to the top of the political agenda. The provision of housing was to become a priority. However, the response of the State to housing need created a new set of problems, to be seen for instance in remote Tallaght and in Ballymun, with their pressing problems of lack of facilities and of isolation in the case of Tallaght. These have been compounded by the problems of high unemployment in these areas.

The Present Situation

The Ireland of the eighties bears many similarities to the Ireland of the mid-fifties. We are again experiencing unemployment and emigration. A lowering birth rate coupled with emigration is leading to a drop in demand for housing. The recession in property and office development combined with the Government grant of £5,000 to Corporation tenants who purchase a new house has shifted house building from the public to the private sector. Half of the units of some blocks of flats have closed up. There are local authority houses vacant in Tallaght and Darndale. Ballymun is slowly being detenanted, with most of its present occupants being single people and single parent families.

The Eastern Health Board is carrying out a pilot resocialisation project in Ballymun with patients from St Brendan's hospital. This resocialisation project could be a pointer towards the way of dealing with people who for one reason or another develop dependency on State or charitable institutions.

Technically there is no need for families to be homeless, squatting or living in hostels. The character of the Corporation approved waiting lists has dramatically changed. In 1968, only 5% of all families on the list had two people in the family unit. Today this has risen to 52.5%.

The transfer list, which is made up of Corporation tenants who wish to move from one area or dwelling to another, had 6,769 applicants in December 1986. In a short time the numbers seeking housing from the Corporation have dramatically declined, yet the numbers who are unhappy with the type of housing which they are in has increased, so that they could be considered to be housed, not 'homed'.

In recent discussion papers the Corporation has recognised two important factors. First, it is largely pointless to expand housing further out to the periphery; people just will not move out there, and future resources available for housing should be concentrated in already built-up areas, particularly in the Inner City where there is an aggregate area of 160 acres (six times the size of St Stephens Green). This figure does not include all the redundant dockland areas as well as the considerable amount of underused land e.g., Grangegorman and various army barracks, as well as many derelict buildings.

Towards the Future

I believe a White Paper must be published immediately. The resources are there to eliminate homelessness; what is needed is knowledge, energy, vision and political will.

Perhaps what is also needed is an inquiry similar to that chaired by Sean T. Ó Ceallaigh, 'The Inquiry into the Housing of the Working Class'. The Inquiry Committee began its public sessions on 29 April 1939 and concluded these sessions in February 1940. It then continued in 1943 with private sessions; it eventually submitted its report in December 1943. What now constitutes housing policy and administration rests on that report.

What I suggest may seem frustrating and long but without the type of actions and struggle which I outlined above, no White Paper will shift the political will of the politicians. I suggest that specific short term objectives which do not need a White Paper should be identified and pursued such as abolition of the vagrancy laws and the changes needed in the distribution of housing stock. This could be done by dialogue with and pressure on politicians. Long term objectives must also be thoroughly examined and pursued with the full participation of groups such as Simon, Focus Point and other community groups. An inquiry such as I described above may be the vehicle for such examination and analysis. The pursuit of short-term and long-term objectives simultaneously but separately may lead to a better and more comprehensive housing policy.

CHAPTER 7

West Tallaght:
a suburban nightmare

West Tallaght Resource Centre

Significant numbers of families availed of the £5,000 grant from the Department of the Environment and moved out of their areas. This has left many houses vacant and run down.

Introduction

With the obvious failure of the Ballymun experiment, high-rise developments came into disrepute, and the Corporation reverted to building houses on the periphery of Dublin in the 'new towns' such as Tallaght and Blanchardstown. The decision to build new towns to the west of Dublin hardly constituted a plan at all. The Corporation has built houses for thousands of families in Tallaght in the 1970s and 1980s, but there has been no authority to oversee the provision of the necessary facilities and services that these families need. The same root problem occurs in West Tallaght as in Ballymun: a fundamental lack of planning beyond the physical planning for the building of houses.

The lessons of the 1960s and Ballymun have not, it seems, been learned, or rather the wrong lessons have been learned. It has been assumed that the problems that arose in Ballymun were due to the high-rise construction and the alleged fact that Irish people do not take to flat-living rather than the true reasons for problems: inadequate facilities and infrastructure, poor integration of different age groups and family types and general lack of social planning.

Precisely these same problems, that first arose in Ballymun, continue to beset Corporation schemes on the outskirts of the city, with the added problems of inaccessibility and poor transport facilities.

This paper will look particularly at the effects of statutory policies as they relate to the development of the large local authority housing estates of West Tallaght. The estates of Killinarden, Jobstown, Brookfield and Fettercairn comprise some 5,000 houses with a population of around 20,000 people. The first houses were built in 1977 in Killinarden and the most recent houses were completed in 1986.

Living in West Tallaght

In considering this issue it is best to begin by trying to give some sense of what life is like for the tenants – the young families, children, single parents – who have come to live in these estates. The vast majority of the housing in West Tallaght is Corporation-owned and the tenants have come from different and often distant parts of the city. They are, by and large, coming to a place that they do not know and have no connections with.

In addition, the area has not always been the first housing choice of these tenants. A sizeable number of them feel that they had no option but to accept a house in West Tallaght, and they experience difficulty in adjusting to a totally new neighbourhood. Living in West Tallaght therefore starts with a disadvantage.

Poor Facilities for Growing Families

Some facilities, particularly schools, have been provided, in the West Tallaght area, but there is a poor and expensive bus system, inadequate shopping facilities and no cinema. Though there is lots of open space there are no developed play areas. There is no health centre, though limited services are made available through parish-owned facilities. There is no Social Welfare office, though the majority of the population depends on social welfare payments as their main or only source of income. There is no local Manpower office, though unemployment in the area is reckoned to be around 70%. There is a Dublin Corporation maintenance depot and rent office, but no housing advice service or rent assessment section. Some of the essential facilities are available in other parts of Tallaght, but they are a bus ride away. Others are available only in the city centre, which is both time-consuming and expensive to reach.

Inadequate Environment

Although the oldest estate in West Tallaght is now nearly ten years old, the whole area still feels, and looks new and unfinished; building went on until very recently and the physical environment is bare and unsightly. The living environment of many families is muddy roadways, earth-filled 'green' spaces, all filled with the noise of JCBs.

West Tallaght is for many, a poor second best. Families cannot be expected to settle and put down roots in an area that is itself unsettled.

Poor Social Mix

Until recently there was no attempt made to provide a mix of housing types in new housing developments. The whole area of West Tallaght consists almost exclusively of standard three and four bedroomed houses, occupied in the main by couples with young families, all with similar needs and pressures. There are very few older people who might provide the informal support and advice that young people who are starting out on family life might appreciate.

A Transit Camp

There are some positive features of life in West Tallaght: the houses themselves are of excellent quality and they all have gardens; and there is a real community spirit in certain areas. But these good points are too frequently outweighed by the lack of services, the experience of isolation and the feeling of living in a transit camp.

In a period of eighteen months during 1986-1987 the effects of the £5,000 grants from the Department of the Environment to local authority tenants who could buy a house in the private sector, have been strongly felt in West Tallaght.

According to a survey conducted between May 1985 and May 1986 by religious groups living and working in the area, significant numbers of families have availed of the grant and moved out. In Fettercairn, out of 700 families, 122 left, all with a member of the family in employment. In Jobstown, out of the 710 families, 113 left, all with a member of the family in employment. This particular policy, which was designed to have a positive effect on the building industry has had a devastating effect on the new, unsettled communities of West Tallaght.

The unemployed and the impoverished are increasingly being ghettoised as the

71

better-off move on. Tenants have had valid concerns about the segregation of their areas and families have been speaking of "being left behind".

Many of the families which availed of the £5,000 grant did so simply because it was a much cheaper way of buying their own house than the tenant purchase scheme at the time. It is significant that some of the families availing of the £5,000 grant remained in the Tallaght area, buying houses in private estates and moving only a couple of miles.

The £5,000 grant has now been abolished in the Budget (March 1987) and thus there should be less movement out of estates in West Tallaght.

The recent revision of the local authority tenant purchase scheme (giving the option to substitute current market value for updated construction cost) now makes it more attractive to tenants in West Tallaght to buy the houses in which they are living.

Allocation of Local Authority Housing

The present points system for the allocation of housing operated by the Corporation has not assisted the development of cohesive communities that tenants can identify with and have pride in. This points system reflects the narrow focus of housing policy with its emphasis on the provision of physical buildings. Points are given for disadvantages like overcrowding and inadequate facilities. But they are not given for social factors, such as proximity to families or friends or to place of employment. These elements may assist their settlement in and satisfaction with the area in which they are housed.

The apparent lack of a long-term policy on tenant purchase has also had a detrimental effect on the estates of West Tallaght. Whole areas, which were originally part of the local authority housing stock, have been purchased by tenants and in many cases resold. There is now a limited number of tenancies potentially available to the housing authority in areas closer to the city centre. Many people express a wish to be housed in these areas.

Reforms

The following immediate and longer-term reforms are required if the quality of life in West Tallaght is to be improved:

Immediate Reforms

1. There are a number of small, relatively inexpensive physical improvements which should be carried out in the various estates in West Tallaght. Estates need to be finished off, paths need to be properly laid, trees planted, play areas provided, green spaces prepared.

2. Recent moves to make the tenant purchase scheme more attractive are to be welcomed. In the context of West Tallaght, where unemployment levels are between 50% and 70%, any tenant purchase scheme should accommodate those

72

on welfare payments. Unfortunately, unemployment is almost a permanent reality and housing policies need to take this into account.

3. There is also an immediate need for the decentralisation of State services to Tallaght. Services of the Department of Social Welfare, Dublin Corporation and Dublin County Council should all be located in this area.

Longer term reforms

1. It is evident from the above that West Tallaght has developed in an uncoordinated way. There is a particular need to propound integrated policies where housing would be just one aspect of a broad-based approach to the needs of people and of communities. Even at this late stage there is a need for some authority to be established and given sufficient powers to initiate and harmonise the various developments required to make Tallaght an attractive town. An authority is needed to link and dovetail the building of houses with the provision of facilities and in turn to coordinate this with transport requirements and other services. The appropriate authority to carry out these tasks is the locally-based new Belgard Council. Where necessary, additional powers and resources should be given to this body so that it can carry out the functions outlined above effectively.

2. The points system should be changed so that local authorities play a more active role in facilitating the development of communities, with extra consideration given to social factors such as the need to house people closer to parents and places of work and to ensure a proper mix of age groups and family types within the estates.

3. Local authorities should physically design housing estates in such way as to enhance neighbourliness and common interests. There seems to be a considerable need for more variety in the type and size of house, in the way they are laid out and in the overall size of estates.

4. The obvious segregation in Tallaght between large private and large public estates suggests that integration of the private and public sector would be more easily achieved through the development of a variety of much smaller estates.

5. It is important that in the future, whole areas and estates of local authority housing stock should not become totally owner-occupied. Tenant purchase schemes should be made as attractive as possible but a significant proportion of local authority housing should be held for renting only.

6. As part of the process of giving more power to the local authority in Tallaght we would like to see an end to the political 'split' between Dublin County Council, Belgard Council and the Corporation. Currently, decisions made by elected Corporation councillors can dramatically affect life in Tallaght, yet Tallaght residents cannot directly and democratically influence this process. Therefore, in any new arrangement the powers of Dublin Corporation need to be significantly reduced.

73

Conclusions

The West Tallaght experience, which is mirrored in other parts of the Dublin suburbs, has clearly shown the difficulties that can arise when housing policies are implemented without reference to the development of policies in other areas which affect people's lives.

The provision of housing, the reduction of the housing waiting list and supports for the construction industry are important initiatives. Housing must however be seen as more than the process of bricks and mortar if we wish to develop communities in which people can develop and live creatively. Urgent consideration must be given to the development of an integrated approach to the planning and establishment of neighbourhoods and communities so that the quality of life for the people in areas like West Tallaght can be improved and the present disastrous experience averted. Ways must be found to allow some sort of constructive dialogue between local people and those who make decisions which affect them. Neither group is able to deal with the issues on their own, but together there may be some possibility of improvement and change.

What is being done: the State's response

This section describes the housing and homeless situation in Dublin as seen by persons working within Dublin Corporation and the Eastern Health Board.

Paddy Morrissey gives historical background including some 'milestones' in Irish housing policy, trends in family size and household type, special needs groups, and the new direction in housing provision.

Pat McDonnell also looks at current trends in policy and housing stock. He condemns decline of the inner city, recommends its rejuvenation and renewal, and the means to achieve the best use of the existing housing stock.

Aidan O'Sullivan gives an explanation of the scheme of priorities for letting, types and sizes of families housed, areas of high and low demand, size of the waiting lists, homeless persons as a special category, conditions and procedure of application.

Christy Geoghegan outlines the work of the Community and Environmental Service of Dublin Corporation and his view of provision for Travelling people, criteria used for assessing need for housing, number housed, type of accommodation provided as well as other aspects of settlement of the Travelling people.

Fred Donohue of the Eastern Health Board describes the role of the Health Boards in providing services for homeless people and sets out proposals for improvements in the Eastern Health Board Region. An integral part of such improvements require co-operation with voluntary organisations.

CHAPTER 8

Current policy and future plans as related to marginal groups

Paddy Morrissey

Dublin Corporation has provided over 76,000 dwellings since 1932.

Housing Policy

Public housing policy in Ireland has followed a remarkably consistent line since the formation of the State. Successive governments have devolved in legislation to local authorities the obligation to house persons who are unable to provide accommodation within their own resources. This condition has been repeated in legislation, regulations and circulars since the 1932 Housing Act. It is restated in the Housing (Miscellaneous Provisions) Bill, 1985.

The other basic requirement for public housing is need. Dublin Corporation has provided over 76,000 dwellings sinced 1932, most of which were originally rented to tenants. Now some 35,000 of these have been purchased and are owner-occupied.

Milestones in Irish housing policy have been as follows:
1. The huge building programmes between 1932-38, 1948-56 and 1967 to date.
2. The introduction of the Differential Rent Scheme in 1950.
3. The economic recession 1955-1959 when for a few years the demand for public housing slackened.
4. The upsurge in demand from the mid 1960s with a rapidly increasing population in the Dublin area.
5. The intensive house building programme from 1968, with an increasing emphasis from the mid 1970s on inner city family houses.
6. The sales scheme introduced in 1968 to enable tenants to purchase their homes.
7. The introduction in 1984 of the £5,000 surrender Grant Scheme (abolished in the March 1987 budget) which with the Housing Finance Agency Loan Scheme enabled local authority tenants to purchase private houses and leave their dwellings available for relettings.
8. The decline in family sizes on the housing list since 1983.

Priorities in Local Authority Allocations

The priority for getting local authority accommodation was always given to families living in insanitary accommodation, including property affected by Compulsory Acquisition Orders, or in overcrowded conditions. Because of the magnitude of the problem (Dublin in the 1920s, '30s and '40s was still a slum city), the major building programmes pre-war and post-war made a significant impression on the housing list numbers only towards the end of the 1950s. The economic recession between 1955 and 1960, when emigration was very high, no doubt also played a part in the fall-off in demand at that time. This decline in demand was a temporary phenomenon.

Within a few short years, the upsurge in the economy and a rapid population growth in the Dublin area saw the waiting lists increasing again and by 1967, the Ballymun scheme was proposed by the Government as a radical solution to the rising demand for local authority housing. Dublin Corporation could not possibly have built the number of dwellings required within the city area because of the scarcity of building land. In the event much of the expanded population was housed in the developing towns in County Dublin – Tallaght, Blanchardstown and Clondalkin. During the mid 1970s the Corporation decided for social reasons to stop building flats in the city and developed inner city sites with family houses. The output of new dwellings remained consistent and between 1967 and 1985 averaged 1,500 units per annum.

Table 8.1   Dublin City Housing List, 1983–1986

Year	Family	Senior Citizens List	Total Housing List
1983	5,420	1,294	6,714
1984	3,921	1,102	5,023
1985	3,648	836	4,484
1986	3,016	735	3,751

Since 1983, however, there has been a continuing decline in the numbers on the city's housing list. This was attributable to a number of factors:

1. The steady annual output of new dwellings over a fifteen-year period.
2. The rapid increase in vacancies for reletting in the estate arising from the operation of the £5,000 grant scheme.
3. The general economic recession.

Not only has there been a fall in the applications but there has been a significant reduction in the family sizes of applicants. The breakdown of family sizes in the most recent review of the housing list on 1 November 1986 is as follows:

Table 8.2   Family Size on the Housing List, 1986

Family size	1	2	3	4	5	6	7	8+	Total
Number	134	1,578	628	328	154	95	30	15	3,061
%	4.5%	52.5%	22.5%	11%	5%	3%	1%	.5%	100%

The demand for dwellings is being readily met by the Corporation in respect of families and allocations are being made to families of two persons and single people. The Dublin housing situation, both in the city and county, is now very much better than it has been since the turn of the century. In many respects, this achievement should not be understated. The cost has been great – total capital debt for housing is now £500 million and the annual loan charges amount to over £50 million.

Housing of Homeless People

The present is therefore a very opportune time to discuss the housing of the homeless groups in the context of the memorandum from Focus Point dated 2 December 1986.*

The effects of the decline in demand and the increased availability of accommodation due to the high rate of vacancies has, over the past year or so, led to an increasing capacity by the Corporation to deal with marginal cases, particularly those classed as 'homeless'. It is significant that Dublin Corporation now has in the Allocations Branch a 'homeless officer'. The Housing (Miscellaneous Provisions) Bill, 1985 sets out to revise and up-date the statutory framework for letting local authority dwellings so as to ensure "that the needs of categories of persons such as the homeless, the aged, the disabled, travellers, etc. get due priority in the formulation of local authority housing programmes". This is a most important legislative step.

This status was subsequently extended to the aged and the itinerants. In this way, great progress was and continues to be made in housing senior citizens and travelling families. The fact that these groups have a special status in law gives them a claim on accommodation and assures their place in Priority Schemes of Allocation. The proposal in the Bill to extend a special status to the homeless will have far reaching effects – particularly if, and no doubt when, there is an increased demand on local authority accommodation. The specific provisions in Sections 8, 9, 10 and 11 of the Bill provide that, in future estimates of housing requirements and annual assessments of needs, housing authorities must have regard to the homeless. They will be required to ensure that suitable accommodation is made available to a homeless person capable of living independently. The housing authority may make arrangements with an approved body for this purpose. The debate on the second stage of the Housing Bill took place in Dáil Éireann on 4 November 1986. The discussion was wide-ranging and almost all points which could be made in relation to housing the homeless were dealt with in that debate.

The number of homeless people housed between May and December 1986 was 1,172. This represented 47% of the total lettings for the period and included 472 families, 316 single parents, 349 single persons, mainly men, and thirty five senior citizens. By any standards this is a most remarkable achievement.

It is wrong to make invalid assumptions that the problem of 'homelessness' in this city is in any way as bad as it is in many other cities including wealthier ones. In fact it is much more manageable. All the more reason therefore to welcome the Bill and to seek to promote its aims by co-operative effort.

*This memorandum proposed the establishment of a Housing Information and Settlement Project as a joint project between Focus Point and Dublin Corporation, co-funded and managed by both organisations. The main objective of the project would be to enable homeless people with particular problems, who need support, to be settled back into the community.

80

CHAPTER 9

The role of the Planning Authority

Pat McDonnell

Mountjoy Square, Dublin, 1988.

Introduction

Dublin Corporation has provided over 76,000 dwellings since the establishment of the State for people who were unable to provide housing from their own resources. A large proportion of these were constructed by Dublin Corporation on serviced green field sites which by today's standards were reasonably close to the city centre. However, many people, whose families had been for generations in the tight, noisy, lively environment of the city centre thought of these new areas as being 'remote'. Certainly, in terms of transport and higher rents there was a problem and it was necessary, in some instances, to persuade people to move there by demonstrating the benefits.

Community amenities in these new areas were rudimentary in the early stages and not organised on a neighbourhood basis. For example, present-day shopping centres in Crumlin are sited almost entirely at junctions and along well-established roads. Schools and churches were few and widely dispersed as they had to cater for a very large population. Crumlin between 1934 and 1939 had more than 3,000 houses erected and 5,400 by 1945. It forms a continuum with a further 3,000 dwellings in Ballyfermot. There is a litany of names of further extensive Corporation housing estates built along the north fringes. The building of these estates has extended right up to the present day.

All of these schemes were a response to the enormous legacy of poor housing which the State inherited in the early days of independence. The highest priority was placed on slum clearance, removal of gross overcrowding and improvement of the health conditions of the people.

The 1930s, 1940s, 1950s and 1960s saw a series of cyclical housing crises with varying responses such as the building of Ballymun. The phase of system-built houses were further examples of providing large numbers of dwellings to cater for the needs at the time. However, due to demographic change, the nature of the traditional demand for public housing had diminished by the early 1980s.

Change in Demand

Dublin Corporation planners have been reviewing the 1980 Dublin Development Plan, which is a statutory duty to be carried out every five years. During the course of investigation the housing waiting list of the Corporation was examined. The list had declined by 25.4% in the three and a half years between May 1981 and November 1984 with the family list declining by 29% and the senior citizens list (i.e. for people over sixty years) by 8.8%.

This resulted in a growing awareness of a need for redefinition of the housing problem. This volume, by focussing specifically on the changed meaning of the term homelessness, is a step in that direction.

The senior citizens' list constituted 14% of the total list in 1977, but by November 1984 it constituted 21.9%, which reflects the city's ageing population generally. By May 1985 the housing list had decreased again to 3,806 on the family list with 1,007 on the senior citizens list. The two largest groups on the family list

82

were two-person (44%) and three-person (30%) households, a total of 75%. Twenty per cent of all families in the inner city are single parent families compared to an 11% proportion in the County Borough. Evidence of a specific need is illustrated by the fact that in 1983 there were 1,840 illegitimate births out of a total of 18,745 births in Dublin City and County. In 1984 one dwelling in every six was being provided for unmarried mothers, who comprised a large percentage of the two-person category on the housing list.

The number of families of three persons and over has declined, and families of six persons or over now constitute less than 5% of the housing list. Household size continues to fall, as does family size. Overcrowding in a nuclear family context likewise continues to decline. The traditional notion of family unit of parent and two, three, four or more children is no longer central or the norm for the Corporation housing list.

Sister Stanislaus has identified a growing number of younger people who gravitate towards the centre of the city without the means or resources to provide housing. 1,500 people went to Focus Point between September 1985 and September 1986. These people do not qualify with adequate points on the housing lists, nor if they do, is the Corporation in a position to provide suitable accommodation. This group very often has to face the additional problems of unemployment and of integration into an existing community. The traditional family of parents and children had been the main component of the housing list. Housing need based on medical or compassionate grounds was a very small part of the list. The 'special needs' definition should now be widened to take account of the growing section of the population, both young and old, mostly single, without the means or resources to provide their own housing.

These, therefore, are features of the demand side of the equation. What has been happening to the supply side of housing, and the existing housing stock?

Housing Supply

Dublin Corporation has not built flats for anyone other than senior citizens since the mid 1970s. The Corporation built approximately 1,500 houses per annum between 1977 and 1984, of which 420 or 27% were built in the County Borough, with the remainder in the County Council area.

Between 1976 and 1984, on average an approximate 200 Corporation nuclear family houses were constructed per annum in the inner city. These houses are red brick, two and three-storey family terrace houses with front and back gardens.

There is naturally an enormous demand for these houses — a demand which can never be satisfied because of shortage of sites and building costs. In contrast, there are a number of vacancies in new housing built in the County Council area, for example, in Tallaght.

No significant activity is taking place in the co-operative housing field, and other forms of intermediate housing arrangements are conspicuously absent.

In the years between 1971 and 1981 there was a loss of over 4,000 privately rented units (unfurnished) – this possibly reflects a contraction of the bedsitter type accommodation. This decline can be expected to continue. There are now large parts of upper floors of premises on city centre streets vacant, places where people formerly lived. These will tend to deteriorate if left vacant. Furthermore, there is an increasingly ageing building stock in the city. For example, 31% of dwellings in the County Borough were built before 1919, with another 22% built between 1919 and 1940. In the inner city the figures are even worse with 53% of dwellings built before 1919. Extensive areas of the inner city and inner suburbs are showing signs of decay.

Community Development and Rejuvenation

It is accepted that the nature of demand and the composition of the housing list has changed. Planners see the potential and necessity to redirect funds to achieve more than a purely housing solution. This would entail less emphasis on newly built housing. There would be much more emphasis on rehabilitation, refurbishment perhaps with starting grants for 'setting-up' (homesteading), urban conservation and area-based renewal. This could all be done within the framework of an inner city community development programme. Planning within a community context would mean a right to more than just a house. The whole question of the wider environment and community facilities would also have to be considered. The premise upon which this proposal is based is the gross under-utilisation of the existing built stock which without a useful life will decay further. What is really needed is a widening of special category needs, and a creative matching of needs with existing available housing or potential opportunities for housing.

As part of the Development Plan Review Process of Dublin Corporation, the possiblity of introducing the concept of a 'rejuvenation area' is being considered i.e. investing resources into some areas of the city which have fallen into decay, so as to restore the physical fabric, thus encouraging economic and community activity.

The past is, in a sense, not relevant. Housing problems were identified and largely satisfied. We need now to respond to the needs of our time.

CHAPTER 10

The allocation of dwellings by Dublin Corporation, particularly to homeless people

Aidan O'Sullivan

Local authority housing in Dublin's North Inner City.

Introduction

This chapter sets out the system of housing allocation which is used by Dublin Corporation. It makes particular reference to homeless people.

How Does the Allocation System Work?

Dublin Corporation dwellings (houses and flats) are allocated in accordance with the Corporation's Scheme of Priorities for Letting of Housing Accommodation. This Scheme sets out the rules which determine who gets a Corporation dwelling. The Scheme is generally referred to as the 'Points Scheme'. The term 'homeless' is used by Dublin Corporation to describe people who do not have adequate points to be allocated a house and who are in need of housing.

Applicants for housing are awarded points which are intended to indicate their need for housing, so that applicants with higher points are deemed to be more in need than people with lower points. Points are awarded for such factors as overcrowding, lack of amenities, sharing facilities with another family, length of time as a housing applicant, health circumstances and so forth. Certain urgent cases are considered for housing without having to have points. Examples of these would be persons displaced from dangerous buildings or rendered homeless by fire or flood.

Before a person can be offered housing, three qualifications must be met:

1. The person must be in need of housing.

2. The person must lack the resources or income necessary to provide his/her own accommodation.

3. The person must be residing in the Dublin area.

The Corporation houses many different types of family unit, i.e., husbands and wives with or without children, single parent families whether these comprise unmarried mothers, separated or deserted wives, widows and widowers. Separated and deserted husbands with custody of children are, of course, eligible for housing but it must be said that comparatively few cases in these categories apply for housing. Senior citizens, that is persons of at least sixty years, are also housed. Certain categories of single persons under sixty years are also considered, i.e., single people who are homeless, generally people over forty years but in certain circumstances persons over twenty years will be considered subject to availability of vacancies. When I refer to a 'family', I mean any grouping of at least two persons who are living together.

Persons are allowed to choose the areas in which they wish to be housed. However, this does not necessarily mean that a person will succeed in obtaining a house in that area. For example, a family which seeks a house in the inner city may not succeed in getting one of these houses as the demand for them is very high compared to the demand for houses in the suburb or county areas. In addition, it is the policy to reserve most of the inner city houses for existing Corporation tenants. These tenants in many cases would comprise large families and would be transferred

86

from overcrowded Corporation flats. The resulting vacancies in the latter flats would be available for the smaller families on the housing list.

People who wish to be housed quickly may decide that their best chance is to list themselves for a house in an area in which there are large numbers of houses available and where the demand is not so high, for example a Corporation house located in a county area – Tallaght, Clondalkin or Blanchardstown.

Housing List and Number of Allocations

The Housing List is revised every six months and at the start of the current List at 1 November, 1986, there were 3,751 applicants on the List as follows:

Dublin Corporation Housing List, 1 November 1986

Family List	3,016
Senior Citizen List	735
	3,751

In recent years the numbers on the Housing List have been falling although there was a slight increase by November 1986 compared to the figure for May, 1986.

The sizes of the family units on the list are also decreasing. For the first time, families of 'size two' (i.e., childless couples or single parents with one child) comprise over 50% of the entire family housing list – the actual proportion is 52.5%. Large families form a very small proportion of the list, with families of six persons or more constituting only 4.5% of the list.

In 1986, approximately 804 single persons who were not senior citizens were housed by the Corporation. These represented 21% of the total number of family units housed in that year. The comparable percentage for 1985 was 14% and for 1982, 8%. This increase indicates that the Corporation is housing an increasing number of single people.

In the year 1986, approximately 3,900 lettings of dwellings were made by the Corporation to persons on the Housing List and to homeless persons and families. In addition, approximately 2,020 Corporation tenants were transferred at their own request from one dwelling to another. This total of 5,920 lettings involved 18,440 persons which meant that in 1985 the Corporation facilitated the movement of a population equivalent to that of a large-sized provincial town.

Homeless Persons and Families

Families who are homeless can be housed very quickly by the Corporation at present. The Scheme of Priorities (Section 10) specifically provides that families claiming that they are homeless may be considered as a matter of urgency for accommodation. At present there is no necessity for a homeless family to enter a hostel as a prelude to being housed. The present situation is that the Corporation has quite a number of vacant dwellings available and any family which is homeless can be accommodated quickly.

87

Sometimes there are complications in cases where families approach the Corporation claiming to be homeless and seeking accommodation. The family may already be tenants of the Corporation and may have left their house, giving some reason why they cannot continue to live there. The Corporation has a system in operation whereby tenants who are not happy with their present dwelling can apply for a transfer to another dwelling. There is a Transfer List for such tenants operating on a Points System, which operates in much the same way as the Housing List. Families may claim to be homeless but it may be the case that one spouse and children are seeking separate accommodation while the other spouse is residing on his/her own in a Corporation dwelling. The background to these cases has to be investigated and often the recommendation of a social worker is sought. If the spouse claiming to be homeless and seeking separate accommodation is already a house-owner or joint-owner, then the case is further complicated. The Corporation sometimes grants temporary lettings until matters of house ownership or family difficulties are resolved. If these matters are not resolved, then the temporary letting is regarded in effect as a permanent letting.

Dwellings provided by the Corporation were originally intended for either families or senior citizens. Smaller flats were not provided specifically to house single people who were not senior citizens. Single people can obviously be only offered small one-room or two-room flats. Flats this size tend to become vacant in large numbers only in areas where there are large flat complexes such as Ballymun for example. Single people tend to be housed in these areas because this is where suitable flats become available.

It may be sometimes thought that the Corporation is deliberately directing *single people* into particular locations, but this is not so. The reason why large numbers of single people are housed in areas like Ballymun is that this is where small flats become available and at present families with children are generally not willing to accept these flats.

In an effort to disperse single homeless people throughout the Corporation's estates, the Housing Committee decided in 1985 to reserve fifty units of accommodation in higher demand areas for single homeless persons over forty years of age. Fifty small flats throughout the entire housing estates were earmarked solely for persons in this category. This experiment has not proved as successful as we would have wished. The reason is that homeless people in general prefer to take the flats that are immediately available in low demand areas rather than wait for a vacancy to arise in one of the fifty reserved flats. A flat under this programme has, of course, to become vacant before it can be designated as a reserved flat and offered to a homeless person.

The Housing Department has a specific officer, the Homeless Officer, who operates from the Allocation Branch.

Single persons claiming to be homeless give different reasons for their homelessness. A common reason nowadays is that the young persons, generally males, cannot get on with their parents at home. Others from the country may be in Dublin for some years, unable to find a flat and end up in a hostel. Others have gone to England for work and when they return either cannot or will not go back to the family home in Dublin. Another reason for seeking accommodation is that persons cannot afford the rent in a private flat. Persons who cannot afford rent are specifically covered by the Scheme of Priorities (Section 22), and will be considered for accommodation. A number of cases in this category have been housed to date.

Persons under threat of eviction from a landlord are also covered by the Priorities Scheme. In fact, these persons are awarded priority status under the Scheme. Generally in these cases the Corporation would require evidence of a Court Order and the Sheriff's warrant. The Corporation is flexible in these matters. In the case of senior citizens, it would not insist that the elderly person goes through the trauma of court proceedings. If there is evidence of a bona fide request by a landlord for possession, the elderly person will be considered at that stage. Basically, no family which has been evicted by a landlord or under threat of eviction will be left homeless by the Corporation.

CHAPTER 11

Community and environmental services by Dublin Corporation

with special reference to Travelling people

Christy Geoghegan

Children playing outside the *tigíns* in Finglas.

Introduction

The Community and Environment Department of Dublin Corporation has a budget of about £40 million and a workforce of about 1,850 people. It differs from other Departments in that the services it delivers are oriented to people as distinct from physical services such as roads and drainage. It attempts to improve the quality of life by removing domestic refuge, street cleaning and the provision of recreational opportunities in parks, swimming pools and sports halls. It seeks out ways and means of promoting self-help and development within the community by helping individual members of the community. In the course of doing this it gives attention to the special needs of minorities in our society. These minorities would include the elderly for whom special arrangements are made to meet their needs. In the same way special arrangements are made to meet the needs of Travellers.

Travellers and Homelessness

Travellers were always classified as homeless for the purpose of rehousing and as such were given a priority. The practice up to the 1960s was to approach the needs of Travellers in much the same way as the approach to meeting the needs of the settled community.

This approach highlighted certain anomalies insofar as Travellers were concerned. Travellers felt threatened and uneasy in an environment which was surrounded by local authority houses occupied by the settled community; there were problems accommodating animals and horse-drawn carts in the areas; and above all, the Travelling people felt the insecurity of being recognised as 'different' from the larger settled community. It became necessary to re-examine the position to place greater emphasis on the difficulties faced by the Travellers themselves and to examine alternative ways of meeting their needs. Accordingly, a special section was set up to cope with the unique issues involved and this was supplemented by a supportive follow-up from a team of welfare officers. However, whereas the homeless are concerned with housing, the Travellers are seeking accommodation which is not necessarily in houses. Nevertheless, it was possible to house 129 travelling families between 1982 and 1986 in the conventional housing stock of Dublin Corporation.

There is still a plentiful supply of such housing available for offer to travelling families provided two criteria have been met. If it were not for these criteria, the housing needs of Travellers could be solved overnight, on paper at least.

The first criterion for travellers is that the travelling families be *recommended* for housing by the Housing Welfare Officer. Because of the early successful approach by the Housing Welfare Officer by which it was found that all Travellers who were prepared to take up conventional local authority housing had done so, there are few, if any, families left that could be recommended.

The second criterion is that the Travellers would take up the offer. Strangely, few Travellers wish to be considered for conventional housing. Their first preference is now almost overwhelmingly in favour of serviced halting sites, or caravan parks as they are now called. These caravan parks serve as a casual introduction to a more settled arrangement for which the Travellers themselves may opt. Their second preference is for group housing schemes, which are an actual consequence of their first preference. While Travellers are provided with halting sites the Corporation try to encourage them to settle in group housing schemes. These are a mixture of bungalows set apart on sites of their own.

In the context of a built-up city there is a formidable task involved in providing sites for this purpose. At present the Corporation has 102 travelling families in group housing schemes and fifty seven families in their caravan parks. There are, however, 120 travelling families on unauthorised sites in the city. Already building plans are in preparation for thirty four families; sites are being examined which could accommodate another sixteen families but there will still be a shortfall for seventy families for whom sites are urgently required. The grave shortage of suitable sites in the city is the first and main problem facing Travellers.

There is certain animosity between Travellers and the settled community. Travellers have to face up to the fact that all members of society have duties as well as rights. One cannot demand rights to the exclusion of duties. By duties I mean normal standards of behaviour and respect for other people's rights. Among Travellers, unfortunately, there is little regard for them and a change of attitude is therefore required.

Future Policies

The Housing (Miscellaneous Provisions) Bill, 1985 includes sections dealing with Travellers which will be helpful in implementing a programme. However, the real issue in the city is the provision of sites and a change of outlook by Travellers themselves. Prejudices in the settled community can be overcome in the long term and this will hinge to a great extent on how Travellers themselves improve their relationship with the settled community. From my own experience, I can detect a slight and welcome improvement.

In the short term, the aims of the Travellers' Section of the Community and Environment Department can be best assisted by the submission to them for examination of any possible site that might be suitable. In the meantime, in order to safeguard the investments made to date in caravan parks and group housing schemes, it will be necessary to introduce a number of Prohibition Orders to prevent unlawful encampments setting up in the general environs of recognised and accepted settlements. Otherwise, the whole programme could be undermined and future developments prejudiced if proper control is not exercised.

The Corporation is conscious of the fact that education is a vital ingredient in any concerted effort to improve the well-being of the Travelling people. Accordingly it has been possible to provide school premises at four of its bungalow sites and training centres at two of these sites. Proposals are under consideration for additional training centres.

Recreational facilities in the form of community halls at four sites have already been provided. These facilities can best be used and provided where there is a sufficient number of families present on any particular site.

With a view to promoting a greater take-up by travelling families of these services outlined above, the appointment of community workers is being considered to supplement the team of social workers who are already working in the field. However, irrespective of legislation or extra staff the challenge of resettlement for travelling families can only be met by the provision of sites which in the built-up areas of the city is very difficult to achieve, but which will be faced up to with determination. The table below illustrates what has been achieved and what now remains to be done to accommodate the homeless Travellers in Dublin city.

Table 11.1 Deposition of Travelling People in Dublin City, 1982-1986

	October 1982	*October 1986*
Number of families living in standard houses	86	129
Number of families living in chalets and group housing	93	102
Number of families living in trailers on authorised sites	56	57
Number of families living on the roadside	38	120

	Units
(a) Under construction, 1986	34
(b) Sites under examination, 1986	16
(c) Number of further sites required, 1986	70
	120

It will be noted that there has been a threefold increase in the demand for sites over the past four years. The programme in 1982 was designed to fully meet the needs of Travellers as they had existed. However, with the continued migration to the city a much expanded programme is now necessary.

CHAPTER 12

The role of the Eastern Health Board in providing services for the homeless

Fred Donohue

At night, young people become vulnerable to the raw exploitation of street life. It is not unusual for them to become involved in crime, male and female prostitution, alcohol and drug abuse.

Introduction

This chapter discusses the role of Health Boards in providing services for the homeless. The first part deals with those over eighteen years of age. The second part deals with children and adolescents aged under eighteen years.

The chapter sets out proposals for improvements in the services for the homeless in the Eastern Health Board region, to be provided by the Board directly or through co-operation with voluntary organisations. The proposals outline a comprehensive service.

Legislative Background

The responsibility of the Health Boards to provide accommodation for, *inter alia* homeless persons is set out in Section 54 of the Health Act, 1953 and the Institutional Assistance Regulations made under that Act. This legislation imposed a duty on a Health Board to provide institutional assistance, i.e. shelter and maintenance, for any person in their functional area who requires it and who is unable to provide it for himself. The regulations allow a Health Board to provide this shelter and maintenance either:

1. in a county home or similar institution maintained directly by the Board;
2. by making arrangements under Section 10 of the Health Act, 1953 (now replaced by Section 26 of the Health Act, 1970) with other organisations for the provision of the service in other institutions.

There has also existed the responsibilty of Local Authorities, as housing authorities, to provide housing for those unable to provide housing for themselves and their families.

This dual responsibility of Health Boards, on the one hand, to provide shelter and mainenance and of Local Authorities, on the other, to provide housing has resulted in a lack of clarity in the definition of the roles of the authorities in providing services for the homeless. It is to be hoped that regulations under the proposed housing legislation will not leave the possibility of continuing ambiguity regarding the responsibilities of Health Boards and Local Authorities in relation to the homeless.

Current Provision

To meet the obligations under Section 54 of the Health Act, 1953, the Board provides an emergency unit for homeless women and children at Brú Chaoimhín. This unit is soon to be relocated at the Regina Coeli hostel. Apart from this unit the Board has, for many years past, provided this service through hostels operated by voluntary organisations, e.g. the Legion of Mary, the Society of St Vincent de Paul, the Iveagh Trust and Family Aid. The Board has supported these organisations through grants and/or payments under Supplementary Welfare Allowance schemes towards the charges made by the various hostels for accommodation. In 1983 a Homeless Unit was set up within the Community

96

Welfare Service to provide a co-ordinated response to those seeking accommodation from the Board. There are two Community Welfare Officers assigned to the Unit under a Superintendant Community Welfare Officer, who is also responsible for the Community Welfare Service for Travellers. While this Unit has provided an excellent and dedicated service in ensuring that accommodation is found for all persons seeking it from the Board, and, where necessary, providing financial support for those availing of this accommodation, it has not been possible to engage in the many other aspects of a comprehensive service for the homeless, e.g. counselling, advice, re-integration into the community and social support.

The Homeless Persons Unit

The present service centres around the Homeless Persons Unit attached to the Community Welfare Service and staffed by two Community Welfare Officers under the supervision of a Superintendent Community Welfare Officer. When a person approaches this unit seeking accommodation, the Community Welfare Officer discusses the need for accommodation with the applicant and endeavours to find the solution best suited to his needs.

The options available are:

1. Facilitate the person to return home;
2. Refer to local authority for housing;
3. Assist the person to avail of private rented accommodation;
4. Refer to emergency unit, Brú Chaoimhín;
5. Arrange hostel accommodation;
6. Arrange other accommodation, e.g. Bed and Breakfast.

At the same time, any necessary financial support through Supplementary Welfare Allowance is arranged. Financial support is continued through this unit while the applicant remains homeless.

An Estimate of the Size of the Problem

At present, on any one night, there are approximately 500 men and 120 women (with seventy children) resident in various hostels in the Eastern Health Board region. These figures do not include the many residents of special hostels (e.g. Dublin Central Mission) who are placed by the Prison, Probation and Psychiatric Services, nor the residents of hostels (e.g. Eglington House). The number of hostel residents fluctuates considerably, tending to decrease during the summer and to increase during the winter.

The trend over the past decade has shown that there has been a steady decline in the number of persons who reside in hostels and indications are that the number will continue to diminish. Among the many contributing factors to this decline in the hostel population are the following:

(a) The policy of Dublin Corporation is to house homeless persons, including single persons, as a priority. The Corporation has, at present, a surplus of accommodation which it is anxious to have occupied.

(b) Rent supplements are available under the Supplementary Welfare Allowance scheme. This means that many people, who would otherwise be homeless, can afford to live in private flats.

(c) Persons approaching the Board for accommodation are discouraged from using hostel accommodation where local authority or private accommodation is a practical alternative. Many persons who would otherwise enter the hostel system are, at that point, persuaded and assisted to remain in the community.

(d) The standard of accommodation in many hostels is poor.

While the hostel population at any one time is approximately 620 adults, the number of persons availing of hostel accommodation over a period is substantially higher. Many only remain in the hostel for one or two nights. On average, twenty five persons per week are being found accommodation through the Homeless Unit of the Community Welfare Service and 2,000 persons per annum are using the service. In addition to those living in hostels there are a number of persons, who for one reason or another, sleep rough. There are varying estimates from various organisations dealing with the homeless as to the number of persons who sleep rough in the Board's area.

On census night, 13 April 1986, the Dublin Simon Community and Focus Point carried out a count of those sleeping rough. On that night, a total of thirty three men and four women were found and this statistic has been formally recorded in the census of population by the Central Statistics Office. This is the first time that the Central Statistics Office has made provision for such statistics.

Table 12.1.

Estimate of the Extent of Homelessness, Eastern Health Board Region, 1986

	Men	Women	Children
Residing in Hostels	500	120	70
Sleeping Rough	33	4	

Periodically various organisations release reports indicating that there are considerable numbers of persons, particularly young persons, homeless and sleeping rough. The above survey did not substantiate these reports. However, the Board has no information from its own sources to either prove or disprove the reports. The absence of up-to-the-minute statistical information makes it very difficult to plan appropriate responses to the homelessness problem.*

*Since this census was taken a survey was carried out by the Eastern Health Board over a three-month period in 1987 which revealed that 386 young people under the age of eighteen years were homeless in Dublin city alone.

Problems in the Present Service

The experience gained over the last three years has shown that, whereas the present service ensures that accommodation is made available to all those over eighteen years who wish to have it, there are many aspects of the service which are not as the Board would wish. There are services considered necessary for a comprehensive service for the homeless which are not always available. The problems and deficiencies in the existing service can be summarised as follows:

Homeless Men

1. While there is more than sufficient hostel accommodation available for homeless men, much of it is below an acceptable standard.
2. Some hostels which are key elements in the service for the homeless are repeatedly under threat of closure.
3. As many hostels require their residents to vacate the premises during the day, there is a need for more and improved day centres offering specialised services for the homeless.
4. Among the homeless population there are a number of 'difficult' cases who have been 'barred' from all available hostels.
5. An adequate and comprehensive follow-up counselling and advice service is badly needed with a view to assisting homeless persons to resume independent living as soon as possible and provide post-hostel support where necessary. The service which is available at present is clearly less than adequate.

Homeless Women and Children

1. At present there is sufficient accommodation available for women and children to meet normal demands. There is, however, little spare accommodation available to meet any increase in demand which may suddenly occur.

    While a good standard of accommodation is provided at the new Family Aid Hostel run by a voluntary committee and will be provided at the new Emergency Unit, the standard of much of the remaining accommodation needs to be raised.
2. At present the Board does not have any control over admission policies to any accommodation other than its own Emergency Unit.
3. While the voluntary bodies involved do exceptional work, a professional counselling and advice service is not always available. It is essential that such a service, properly co-ordinated, be available to re-integrate homeless women and children with their families in the community. Many women and children who approach the Homeless Unit are often very distressed. Such cases require a great deal of time and attention and may require such service immediately.

Homeless Young Persons (Male, 18-20 years)

At present, homeless young males aged between eighteen years and twenty years are dealt with in the same manner and through the same facilities as older persons. Such young persons will only be referred to hostel accommodation as a last resort, but because of lack of alternative facilities, many have to be so referred. Many homeless young persons are immature, are not 'street-wise' and are often very frightened by their predicament. These young persons need a high level of support which is not available for them separately from the hostel system.

Homeless Girls

Experience would indicate that there is sufficient accommodation available for homeless girls. The standard is good and there is no expressed concern about, or deficiencies perceived in, the present situation. When the priority areas identified above have been dealt with, this part of the service can be further examined.

Homeless Couples and Families

Couples or families who become homeless do not frequently approach the Board seeking accommodation. Where this occurs, short-term bed and breakfast arrangements have been found to meet the situation effectively.

How the Service should be Developed

The development of the service to meet the perceived need for a comprehensive service, to overcome the problems and meet the deficiencies which have been identified above is now considered.

Structure of the Proposed Service

The structure proposed for an expanded and developed service for the homeless is to have the following elements:

1. Homeless Unit attached to Community Welfare Service with associated Social Work Service and Out-Reach Service.
2. Two accommodation units directly run by the Board.
   (i) | A 24-hour emergency unit for women and children
   (ii) A short-stay unit for young male persons in the 18-20 year age group. This unit could be associated with a unit for youths under eighteen years.
3. A system of hostels, of suitably upgraded standard, providing short, medium and long-stay accommodation. These hostels would continue to be run by voluntary organisations appropriately supported by the Board.
4. Continuous liaison between Health Boards and local authorities to ensure that housing is provided where appropriate.
5. In-depth assessment of each case coming into contact with the service, with follow-up counselling service leading to re-integration into the community as soon as possible. This service would aim, not only at dealing with the immediate

problem of homelessness, but also at dealing with the underlying problems which in very many cases have caused homelessness. It is also envisaged that, in some cases, support would continue to be required after the homeless person has been re-integrated into the community. Re-integration may take the forms of rejoining the family home, being housed by the local authority or acquiring private rented accommodation.

Staff required

(a) Community Welfare Homeless Unit

    1 Superintendent Community Welfare Officer
    4 Community Welfare Officers
    1 Administrator
    1 Clerical Assistant
    1 Porter

(b) Social Work Service

    3 Social Workers

with attachment to appropriate social work team for homeless young persons

(c) Outreach Service

    2 Outreach Workers

(d) Emergency Unit

    1 Supervisor
    1 Assistant Supervisor
    4 Attendants
    1 Porter

(e) Short Term Unit

    1 Supervisor
    1 Assistant Supervisor
    4 Care Staff
    1 Porter

27 Total

Of the above **27** staff posts required, **7** are available at present.

Other resources required

(a) Sufficient finance to acquire and furnish a suitable building for a short term unit for twelve young males aged 18 - 20 years. This unit should comprise separate sleeping accommodation for each resident, and administrative officer.

(b) Running costs for the short term unit.

(c) Sufficient finance to engage in a comprehensive programme of upgrading for much of the existing hostel accommodation. This programme should include major improvement in the standard of sleeping accommodation and day facilities.

Appendix 12.1 sets out details of the proposed service.

Services for Homeless Persons Under Eighteen Years

There has been continuing concern that care services for those aged between eleven and eighteen years may be less than adequate. The Eastern Health Board's social workers are continuously faced with the problem of arranging placements for this age group and appropriate placements are not always possible. Our social work teams regularly have at least one or two young people as clients who are living rough on the streets or have done so in the past.

Survival on the streets demands that the young person adapts to a pattern of 'street living'. This form of identity and behaviour, once established, is extremely difficult to change and evidence throughout Europe has shown that night shelters do not help to resolve the situation.

Many young people leave home because of a breakdown in family relationships of one sort or another. In some instances this can be a temporary crisis (caused by illness, unemployment or adolescent problems) and if given support and help at the time of the crisis, this family can be assisted to resolve family problems and continue to carry on 'normal life' as before. In other instances, leaving home comes as the final crisis in a family that has had difficulty throughout its history and children leave home as soon as they are old enough to run away. It has been found that many homeless children who had manifested problems in their community by, for example, mitching from school were not brought to the attention of the social services. Appropriate intervention at this earlier stage might have prevented subsequent homelessness. Social work and child care services need to become involved with these families as soon as a problem starts arising.

Furthermore, many of these young people who 'live on the streets' have been, or are in care, but have not been helped to bridge the gap between the 'care situation' and independent living.

When young people are returning home or moving into independent living accommodation from *any* residential care setting, intensive support is needed. This transition period can be particularly difficult when the young person has been in residential care for a considerable time and has little experience of the strains and demands of family life and of independent living. Intensive support, if given, could help prevent homelessness in these instances and help the young person maintain some self-esteem.

102

The Board would envisage that there should be a wide range of services available to meet the needs of this group, who are not adequately catered for either by residential or community services at present. These services should be properly integrated and planned and should include community resources such as family resource centres/drop in centres where the focus would be to help adolescents and families in their own community. There is a need to look at the provision of 'intermediate treatment' as an option for some of these young people. Also, the fostering service should be expanded to include professional fostering which has been successful as a resource for adolescents in other countries. We need to look at the provision of residential care to meet the needs of this age group. There is no residential 'treatment centre' at present and many of the existing facilities are not in a position to cater for adolescents and their problems. Indeed, regrettably they will often not accept referrals of 'difficult' boys and girls over twelve. It is also becoming increasingly apparent that residential care workers are facing extremely difficult and demanding situations when dealing with young people in care and these issues need to be addressed when planning services, recruiting and training staff.

For example, they often have to deal with very difficult acting-out behaviour, sexual issues, school refusal and other school problems, poor self-esteem and coping skills and so forth. Finally, there is a need for a short term hostel which would be an integral part of the services for adolescents. This should cater for 10-12 young people and include emergency places. It is vitally important that this accommodation be of a high regard, and not a convenient alternative to the street. The hostel should be located where it is convenient for children and others faced with an emergency situation and where families can have access to the service when their child is in the care of the hostel. Central location would facilitate children continuing at their own school and availing of other services.

An Outline of the New Hostel

The hostel programme would have a programme for each individual resident. The programmes must have the flexibility to deal with the individuality of each person. There would be a high level of individual counselling and group work, within day-to-day activities. The programmes would include continuous reviews of their appropriateness to the children placed in the hostel.

Following the admission of a child to the hostel, a programme for resolving that child's difficulties would be worked out with him. There should be an 'intake' meeting for all those who currently know or work with the child, and/or child's family, within the first week of the child's admission to ensure that all information is gathered as soon as possible so that the best plan may be made for the child. This would involve consultation with all other agencies currently involved with the child. Each child should be reviewed throughout his or her stay so that the work being carried out would be appropriate to the needs. Contact with the children and families should be an integral part of this work.

103

The Social Work Role

Because of the short term nature of the hostel, intensive social work would be required. Close liaison with staff and the willingness to share tasks would be essential during placement in order to ensure that results are achieved. The child's social worker would be part of the review system on planning for the child's future. The emphasis in the programme would be on a reconciliation with the child's family so that the child could return as quickly as possible to live at home. For some children this will not be possible and long term placement would have to be sought in the most appropriate setting for the child, e.g., long term foster care, residential care, hostel care or special residential care.

Staff of the Hostel

The most crucial element of the hostel would be its staff. A high ratio of staff to residents would be necessary due to the intense nature of the work. There should be enough staff to provide a 24-hour service with a minimum of two staff members per shift. Staff selected would have to have the ability and desire to work as a team. The team would comprise a variety of skills and disciplines. Training of staff on an on-going basis would be essential, as an integrated part of the programme.

After Care

After care should not be seen as a separate service. It would be an integral part of the whole short term programme. The essential ingredients of an effective after care service are variety and a range of supportive back-up services.

Management Structure of the Hostel

A Board of Management would be appointed to work for the hostel. The main criteria for appointment should be experience in dealing with the problems encountered by young people and a sound knowledge of and ability to manage such a hostel. Policy should be devised in conjunction with staff.

Consultants to the Hostel

As a complement to the skills of the staff, a team of professionals from various disciplines should be available as required in each case. This would include a psychologist, psychiatrist, paediatrician and social worker, for example. These individuals would have an identity with the hostel and, when required, would assess children within the hostel rather than in the clinical surroundings of hospitals and clinics.

Evaluation of the Hostel

The hostel must have a system of evaluation built in so that its progress is monitored in relation to the problems of homeless children.

Framework for Services for Young People

It is vital that all services for children at risk are properly co-ordinated and

Fig. 12.1 Eastern Health Board Framework for Development of Services

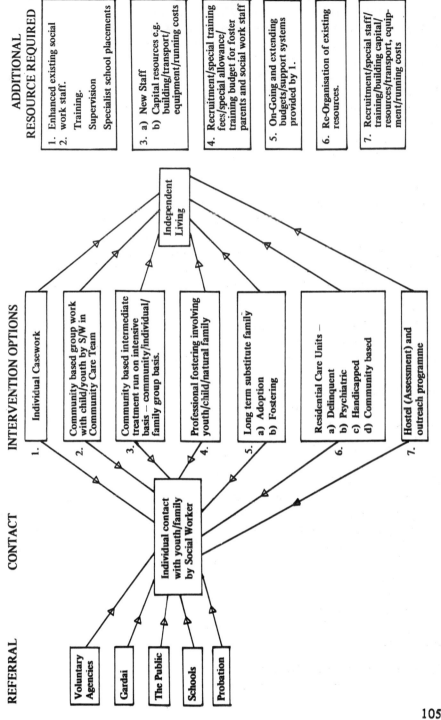

REFERRAL   CONTACT   INTERVENTION OPTIONS   ADDITIONAL RESOURCE REQUIRED

1. Individual Casework

2. Community based group work with child/youth by S/W in Community Care Team

3. Community based intermediate treatment run on intensive basis — community/individual/family group basis.

4. Professional fostering involving youth/child/natural family

5. Long term substitute family
   a) Adoption
   b) Fostering

6. Residential Care Units —
   a) Delinquent
   b) Psychiatric
   c) Handicapped
   d) Community based

7. Hostel (Assessment) and outreach programme

Independent Living

Individual contact with youth/family by Social Worker

Voluntary Agencies

Gardai

The Public

Schools

Probation

1. Enhanced existing social work staff.
2. Training.
   Supervision
   Specialist school placements

3. a) New Staff
   b) Capital resources e.g. building/transport/equipment/running costs

4. Recruitment/special training fees/special allowance/training budget for foster parents and social work staff

5. On-Going and extending budgets/support systems provided by 1.

6. Re-Organisation of existing resources.

7. Recruitment/special staff/training/building capital/resources/transport, equipment/running costs

planned within a philosophy of care. Whether or not these services will be provided by the Health Board itself or contracted out to other agencies or voluntary bodies, who are often not accountable to the Health Board and who, in general, reserve the right to accept or refuse a child to the service, must be considered. Accountability must be to the Health Board if it is substantially funding a service. Matters such as admission criteria and the policy of each facility are very relevant in this regard. Planning the overall framework of the services and how they fit in with each other is also important.

Fig. 12.1 sets out a framework for the development of social work and social services to young people at risk. These are divided between services focussed on helping the young person in his own home and community, (options 1 to 3) and services which provide an alternative to his own home for the young person (options 4 to 7). The options are now outlined as follows.

Option 1 — Individual Casework

When a child or a young person with personal or social difficulties is referred to the area team, the initial point of contact would be with the community care social worker, who would make an initial investigation and assessment of the young person and his/her family situation. From this it could be determined where in our continuum of care, i.e., treatment options set out in the chart, the most appropriate point of intervention resides. The community care social worker will remain responsible for the planning and reviewing of the work undertaken. In line with policy, the first priority must be to maintain the young person within their own family and community wherever possible. In certain cases, one-to-one contact by a social worker with the young person and his/her family may provide enough support to achieve this.

Option 2 — Community Based Group Work

Individual work with young people is often enhanced by group work and this is an option that needs to be developed within the present community care structures.

In particular, this would be an important addition to the working with young people on supervision orders (as envisaged in the Children's Bill, 1985). Since social workers are currently using group work as a technique with young people, there is a need to develop and expand the use of these skills in a cohesive way.

Option 3 — Community Based Intermediate Treatment

Intermediate treatment is a term used to describe programmes of work which are specifically arranged for young people in trouble or at risk in the community. As such, it is part of the services for young people which aim to help them within their own environment and so avoid the need for residential care. In practice, particular attitudes and methods of work have come to be associated with the term. For example, every effort is made to obtain the trust and confidence of the young person who may be highly suspicious of, and even hostile to, authority. Group work is generally a regular feature of intermediate treatment and involves encouraging discussion among the young people in an effort to help them understand themselves and explore their way towards accepted standards of behaviour. Activities may include weekends or longer periods at various centres where adventure activities are used to extend the child's experience and give him/her the opportunity to co-operate actively with other young people and adults. Other activities follow a similar pattern to those found in youth clubs. The philosophy of intermediate treatment is in line with good social work practice with children and young people and it should not be seen as an isolated operation separated from other child care practices.

Option 4 — Professional Fostering

Experience of professional fostering in other countries has shown that many of the most troublesome teenagers in care can be looked after in the community. This type of scheme should be one of the alternatives available to adolescents who cannot remain with their own family. The concept is basically one of 'treating' severe problems of young people in a family setting where the young person can be helped to fit back into their own family or more successfully into adult society. It is important to remember that professional fostering aims to solve problems and is not a substitute home. These foster parents are paid a professional fee (£80 – £100 at 1986 prices) per child per week in addition to the fostering allowance by the Eastern Health Board. Each placement is contract based and this is agreed with the young person, foster family, agency and natural parents.

Option 5 — Long Term Substitute Families

Adoption

It is to be hoped that with future changes in legislation, adoption will become a choice for a much wider range of children who are in need of permanent families in the future. This would be a welcome option for adolescents who want this choice.

Long term Fostering

There has been a history of placing children in long term foster care in the Eastern Health Board. More recently, the Board has placed a number of young people over eleven years of age in foster families. There will be a continuing need for this type of placement. We note that it is increasingly difficult to recruit foster families and this will have to be addressed.

It is recommended that relatives should be considered as foster families where possible, as recent research in England has shown that this is the most successful type of family placement for children/young people.

Option 6 — Residential Care

Residential care will best meet the needs of some of this age group, particularly of some of those who are difficult and disturbed and cannot remain in their own homes. However, many of the existing facilities are not in a position to cater for adolescents and their problems. Indeed, regrettably, they will often not accept referrals of 'difficult' boys and girls over twelve years of age. It is also becoming increasingly apparent that residential care workers are facing extremely demanding situations and these issues need to be addressed when planning services and recruiting and training staff. As there are considerable residential resources already in existence, the task here is to co-ordinate and, if necessary, redefine the residential services in order to meet current needs and to work out an overall plan with the different voluntary bodies involved in this field.

Option 7 — Hostel (Assessment) Programme

There is a need, as outlined above, for a short term assessment hostel, the focus of which would be intensive work with the young person and his/her family. It must be obvious from all this that services for children and young people need to be properly planned and co-ordinated in a systematic way and not developed on an ad hoc basis or in response to any particular crisis. Within the continuum of care as outlined in this chapter, some of the resources required are already in existence, e.g., community care social workers, long term foster families and residential care. These need to be enhanced and expanded.

However, some of the options described would need new development within the Eastern Health Board, e.g., community based intermediate treatment, professional fostering and the short term hostel programme.

In this chapter a proposal for the improvement of services and for a comprehensive service for the homeless by the Eastern Health Board is set out, to be provided directly through the Eastern Health Board itself or through co-operation with voluntary organisations.

A crucial issue throughout the range of services provided by the Health Board would be that of review and evaluation. It is vital to ensure that each of the treatment options continues to meet the needs of their target groups and is modified or developed in line with changing needs. Through evaluation reports and review structures, each section of the proposed service would be accountable to the Health Board who would maintain overall responsibility for the provision of the total service.

Appendix 12.1
Proposed Service for Homeless Persons over Eighteen Years

1. *Community Welfare Homeless Unit*
   The proposed service will be centred in and controlled from an expanded Homeless Unit attached to the Community Welfare Service. This unit will be responsible for developing, organising and running the service and for the development and implementation of overall policy re the homeless. It will also be responsible for securing the appropriate type of accommodation for each homeless person, in consultation with the Social Work Service where necessary, and for providing any necessary financial support through Supplementary Welfare Allowance.

2. *Referral Agencies*
   Homeless persons will be referred to the Homeless Unit by many agencies including:
   Self-referral; Prisons and Probation Service; Gardai, Clergy and other community figures; Psychiatric Hospitals; General Hospitals; Health Board Staff e.g. Public Health Nurses, Area Social Workers; Voluntary organisations e.g. Focus Point, Simon Community, Society of St. Vincent de Paul.

3. *Out-reach Service*
   So that the Board's service would not merely be a response to persons seeking accommodation but would take positive steps to seek out homeless persons, it is proposed that the Board would employ Outreach workers. It would be the function of this service to actively endeavour to make contact with homeless persons who, for whatever reason, do not approach the Homeless Unit. On making contact the Outreach worker would himself make the referral. It would also be the function of the Outreach service to confirm and monitor the numbers and locations of persons sleeping rough.

4. *Social Work Service for the Homeless*
   The homeless Unit should have available to it a specialised Social Work Service providing services exclusively for the homeless. The main function of this service would be:

   (a) To provide, where necessary, an assessment service when a homeless person first makes contact with the Homeless Unit.

   (b) To provide social work services for those referred to the Emergency Unit or the Short-Term Unit for Young Persons.

   (c) To provide, where necessary, social work services for persons referred to the general hostel system.

109

(d) To provide, where necessary, continuing support services for homeless persons who have been re-integrated into the community.

5. *Emergency Unit for Women and Children*

This unit is presently located at Brú Chaoimhín. It will shortly be relocated at the Regina Coeli Hostel. The new unit will provide accommodation for up to five families at any one time and will be staffed and run directly by the Board. The unit will have available to it the specialised Social Work Service for the homeless to provide counselling and support. It is essential that families do not remain in this unit for more than a few days but quickly pass on to the General Hostel system or are quickly re-integrated into the community.

6. *General Hostel System*

This system should continue to be operated by voluntary organisations who have developed considerable expertise in this area. The service of the specialised Social Work Service and/or the Community Welfare Service should be available to any residents of the hostels who can be, and wish to be, assisted in being re-integrated into the community.

There are sufficient hostel places available are present though it would be beneficial if some places presently available for males could be made available for women and children. Considerable resources need to be invested in most of these hostels, which are located in very old buildings, in bringing the standard of the hostel accommodation up to an acceptable level.

The Board should continue to support the hostels through Section 65 Grants and/or per capita payments through Supplementary Welfare Allowance. An appropriate mechanism to co-ordinate the overall provision of hostel services needs to be developed.

7. *Short-Term Unit for 18-20 year old males*

The general hostel system is, in many cases, not suitable for young men aged 18-20 years. It is proposed that the Board should acquire, staff and run directly a unit which would provide accommodation for twelve persons in this age group. This unit would have available to it the specialised Social Work Service for the homeless to provide counselling and support. Persons should only remain in this unit for a short period (a number of weeks at most) while being guided towards re-integration in the community.

8. *Bed & Breakfast*

Community Welfare Officers will continue to utilise Bed & Breakfast accommodation in appropriate cases, particularly where families require short-term accommodation.

9. *Re-integration into the Community*

The Board's objective will be to re-integrate people into the Community as quickly as possible. To this end the Community Welfare staff and the specialised Social Work Service will work on an ongoing basis with the residents of the two units directly operated by the Board and of the general hostel system. The desired objective will be to see the homeless person re-united with the family, where appropriate. If this is not appropriate, or cannot be achieved, the homeless person will be encouraged to resume independent living in local authority housing or in private rented accommodation. A number of homeless persons will continue to need a support service after they have been re-integrated into the community.

How the situation can be improved

While there have been dramatic improvements in general housing conditions in Ireland over the last few decades, the very marked emphasis on encouraging owner occupation and on the provision of rented local authority housing has resulted in a very narrow, restrictive and non-innovative view of housing policy, and the eclipsing of the needs of certain marginalised groups. The six chapters in this section suggest possibilities for a more innovative and efficient housing policy as well as identifying the need for a more realistic acceptance of the housing rights and special needs of certain social groups and for homeless people.

Bernard Thompson points to the success elsewhere of voluntary and co-operative housing schemes. Cormac Ó Dúlacháin holds out the prospect of revitalisation of the private rented sector as a potential resource for the housing of vulnerable groups.

Philip Geoghegan, while acknowledging the current financial constraints, argues for a policy of a limited amount of new housing plus an intelligent adaptation of existing housing stock to alleviate the problem of homelessness. These three papers all consider the role of voluntary agencies and associations to be a vital resource in the future development of housing policy.

Michael Mernagh's paper tells the story of how one voluntary group in Dublin's Inner City managed, by dint of commitment and insistence, to have a profound say in the shaping of developing plans in their area. Dick Shannon explains the background to the Housing (Miscellaneous Provisions) Bill, 1985. Stanislaus Kennedy and Justin O'Brien describe how Focus Point is actively exploring a comprehensive settlement strategy for people who are homeless in Dublin city.

CHAPTER 13

Social housing

Bernard Thompson

Many social housing organisations have led the way in meeting the special needs of elderly people, handicapped and other socially vulnerable categories.
Bethany House, Sandymount, Dublin, 1988.

The term 'social housing' is used to describe the movement motivated by mutual and co-operative interest or voluntary philanthropic principles to meet specific housing needs identified by the founders or sponsors of the organisations or 'housing associations' involved in this work. It covers non-profit, cooperative and voluntary housing.

While the constitutional and management structures of these organisations may vary from one country to another and even within countries, their common characteristic is that they are 'non-profit housing enterprises'.

The housing associations which are formed on the basis of co-operative interest function for the mutual benefit of their members who are the tenants or occupiers. Their management structures are based on the involvement of the member/tenants in the decision-making arrangements. The local housing co-operatives are often linked together, through their association, for common services and representation.

Housing associations which function on a voluntary philanthropic basis are organised by management committees who arrange the provision of housing services for others, particularly those with special needs such as the elderly or handicapped.

The social housing organisations have been significant employers of building contractors, technical professions, administrators and welfare personnel. In some instances the largest of them, such as those formed in Sweden and Denmark, originally had a dual purpose: to provide good housing with security of tenure for members (mainly apartments) and to create construction employment. In several countries the trade union movement was involved as the original sponsors of the most highly developed co-operative housing associations now established some forty years. But some of the housing organisations date back to the last century and were started in response to the insanitary and slum housing conditions facing low income workers and poor people following the industrial revolution.

In several European countries the provision of public housing is organised by companies controlled by management boards delegated by the local public authorities, but these are perceived as a separate sector and would correspond to local authority (public) housing in Ireland.

Many social housing organisations operate on a relatively small scale with local and voluntary management boards. In some countries they have led the way in meeting the 'special needs' of elderly persons, handicapped persons or other socially vulnerable categories.

This has been achieved by combining housing provision and management with social supports, welfare and even to some extent para-medical services in an integrated structure to serve the needs of the tenants. In many cases the housing organisations have links with voluntary caring bodies, referral services or church bodies.

In this context the term 'social housing' takes on a deeper and more significant meaning involving the development of a housing stock designed specifically to cater for various special categories in the population and including a system of management which is sensitive to their needs.

In Britain, for example, the voluntary housing movement now provides some 70,000 rental dwellings in sheltered housing schemes of this type to cater for elderly persons. More recently, specially designed housing has been provided for socially vulnerable, handicapped and homeless people. This 'community care' approach to housing frequently involves partnerships with organisations such as MIND, MenCap, Cyrenians, Women's Aid etc. and also the statutory health or housing authorities. Similar approaches have emerged in other countries and, indeed, are becoming an accepted and essential part of developed housing systems.

Community Benefit

Social housing contributes a stock of housing mainly, but not entirely, in rental forms of tenure which is owned for the benefit of the community and the persons who use this form of accommodation. While the organisations involved in its provision and management may cater for a range of income groups and different needs, their emphasis on housing those with limited, low or very low incomes has meant that governments have recognised that these housing services are worthy of State support with capital loans, interest subsidies and grants, etc. In several countries, housing associations or voluntary and co-operative organisations involved in the management of housing, have formed an effective partnership with State and local authorities. This source of housing can be seen as a distinct sector in the national housing systems.

The social housing sector (comprising the various types of housing associations or non-profit housing enterprises) contributes 3% in Britain and between 10% and 20% of the housing stock in several other European countries. In Canada since the end of the 1960s some 35,000 dwellings have been built by co-operatives following the introduction of a finance scheme to assist their development. In summary, therefore, social housing may be described as follows:

1. A mainly decentralised housing provision and management system.

2. A housing system which involves communities, voluntary services and self-help groups in the process of housing provision and management.

3. A means to integrate housing and social or welfare support facilities in a single localised management system.

4. A means to develop 'special needs' housing services for the elderly, handicapped, homeless people or other socially vulnerable groups in their communities.

5. A means to facilitate and encourage tenant self-help and participation in the management of their own housing, depending on the type of organisation and its management system.

6. The facilitation of a wider choice of housing and tenure arrangements than just

117

individual home-ownership or public rental housing, thereby achieving a more balanced housing system and one more sensitive to people's needs.

7. The facilitation of a flexible partnership between statutory bodies and voluntary or co-operative organisations in tackling special housing needs, urban housing renewal, and tenant participation in housing management.

The Limitations of Current Housing Policy

Ireland has not shared to any significant degree in the development of the social housing movement which has successfully emerged in several European and other countries during the past twenty to forty years. While not a panacea for all housing problems, this movement has contributed to a more balanced housing system than exists in Ireland at present.

A reliance on a policy of new house-building, funded directly by the State, but organised and administered by the local authorities under the priorities which are determined in housing legislation, particularly the 1966 Housing Act, has characterised Ireland's efforts to achieve a general improvement in the housing standards of low income groups.

This has been combined with a strong emphasis on support for individual home-ownership, with housing estates built in the suburbs of the towns and cities, assisted by State grants, loans and tax reliefs available to individual purchasers. This approach has been facilitated by the availability of mortgage funds from the Building Societies and the development of 'green field' sites for housing. While a high level of satisfaction has been achieved through access to home ownership, current housing policy has also resulted in the following:

1. The placing of a primary emphasis on satisfying family housing needs.

2. A continued decline in the private rental sector (unfurnished dwellings) which has received virtually no subsidy support for its tenants and which include some of the poorest sections of the population.

3. A fall in the populations of the core areas of the cities and even of the large towns due to suburbanisation.

4. A distortion in the way housing subsidies benefit various income groups with some ambiguity as to the purpose of such subsidies, as between supporting the construction industry, giving access to housing for low and limited income groups, and distributing wealth in housing through tax reliefs.

While the basic housing standards have significantly improved for the population as a whole, certain marginal groups have not shared in this improvement, e.g. the homeless and the elderly poor. New housing needs have emerged − caused by, for example, the increase in single parent families, young single people and the elderly living alone − which indicate the lack of choice or the limited range of housing solutions available in Ireland.

The fact that rental housing, or housing with other forms of tenure and management apart from home-ownership or local authority housing, has not been

118

adequately encouraged has had a direct effect on the flexibility of the housing system to cope with changing economic and social circumstances and has contributed to the decline of the inner city communities.

Examples of the changing housing needs have been signalled by the reports published in recent years. Baker and O'Brien (1979) called for a re-orientation of housing policy from one of responsibility for families to one of responsibility for people and for a restructuring of the financial flow between the public authorities and the housing system. The National Council for the Aged (1984) has also called for a more diverse range of housing in Ireland as a means to achieve mobility from one type of housing to another as circumstances change. For example, a larger stock of sheltered housing with social supports will be needed as the proportion of frail elderly in the population grows. Voluntary housing associations are identified as having a useful contribution to make in this regard if more adequate supports are provided.

In the Report of the Department of Health (1984), policies aimed at encouraging the more widespread application of 'community care' rather than institutional care for a range of socially vulnerable persons were identified. Its recommendations will require the allocation of resources to assist the development of new types of housing service.

Additional problems have emerged as the result of the building of large-scale housing estates by local authorities which have tenants consisting mainly of low income groups who are now subject to the additional stress caused by widespread unemployment. This raises questions about the whole strategy of large-scale housing developments to cater for particular income categories.

The problem of unemployment is also affecting those house purchasers, mainly younger married couples with families, who are now unemployed and cannot afford high mortgage repayments. It is fair to point out that they have had little option but to seek access to home-ownership as no other housing solution with secure tenure and decent standards has been readily available to them.

The underlying problem in Irish housing policy is that it takes too simplified an approach to what is a diverse and complex range of needs. These needs require a multi-purpose housing policy for the organisation and delivery of a range of housing solutions to suit different and changing requirements.

The Development of Social Housing in Ireland

State support for social housing organisations has been a peripheral aspect of housing policy. For example, the provision of capital funding for housing associations, as legal entities, has only emerged since the early 1980s and is confined to housing for designated 'disadvantaged' categories.

This means that there are still serious obstacles in the way of gaining the benefit of organised housing management through the co-operative ownership of housing, particularly apartment housing in urban areas, by members who are not in the disadvantaged categories but for whom this type of housing solution is suitable and acceptable. This form of housing has been successfully organised and financed in many other countries. The introduction of tax incentives to encourage redevelopment has, in the housing context, really only increased the housing choice of those who have large enough incomes to achieve access to upmarket housing.

The lower income groups, the industrial and service workers, are forced to house themselves in the suburbs. Those with special needs who need support services to live independently in suitable housing – a characteristic of the population in all large cities – are forced to depend on institutions or hostels or take poor private rental or local authority housing where they have difficulty in coping on their own. The contribution which social housing organisations could make to overcome the loss of the private rental sector has not been realised.

This does not mean that attempts have not been made to initiate social housing or a 'third arm' in the housing system. Indeed, non-profit rental housing projects have been built by voluntary organisations or trusts, some of which date from the beginning of this century. Since the 1960s, local voluntary groups have built housing mainly for the elderly, using charitable funding and the limited local authority assistance available. Their contributions, although making a useful impact at local level, comprises less than 1% of national housing stock. Research carried out for The Housing Centre in 1983 indicated that about 1,800 dwellings were rented out by voluntary organisations of which about 1,100 were rented to elderly persons. This includes the Iveagh Trust housing stock of 800 dwellings in the Dublin area. But the number of dwellings being built at present by non-profit/voluntary housing groups is increasing, with projects being undertaken in sixteen counties.

Legislative powers for direct public capital and other assistance to 'approved bodies' were provided for in Section 12 of the 1966 Housing Act. Financial assistance under this section was largely dependent on the willingness of local authorities to meet such requests from their own resources. This was only forthcoming on a very limited basis. Therefore, the building of rental housing by non-profit/voluntary organisations has in the past depended to a very large extent on charitable funding or private sources of finance. In these circumstances it is not surprising that output has been small and has largely consisted of 'one off' projects.

Improvements were made in the state assistance in 1979, 1981 and in a more far-reaching way in 1984 when a new capital mortgage and subsidy scheme was introduced to assist 'approved bodies' e.g. non-profit, co-operative and voluntary organisations (or housing associations) with the provision of rental accommodation for low income elderly and other disadvantaged persons including homeless people since 1985. The funding assistance is recouped to local authorities, which receive applications from approved organisations, by the Department of Environment. The loan charges payable by the borrowing organisations are fully subsidised, therefore, the capital assistance has all the characteristics of a grant but legally is a mortgage loan requiring the preparation of legal documentation, etc., for this purpose.*

120

While the introduction of the new capital assistance scheme in 1984 was a significant step in policy development by the Department in the area of encouraging social housing organisations, it has several limitations.

The capital assistance is limited to 80% of the gross cost of projects with a maximum payment of £20,000 per dwelling unit. The approach of the Department to this type of housing, to date, has been to require a high level of *charitable* funding, amounting to 20% of the cost of projects. The scheme has been a source of encouragement to organisations in a position to raise funds or obtain donated sites and buildings, particularly those catering for the elderly.

The capital assistance is confined to approved organisations housing mainly 'disadvantaged' persons – low income elderly, the homeless, the handicapped, single parents and families on local authority approved waiting lists. Local authorities would receive 100% capital assistance to house the same categories.

Capital assistance of 95% would be appropriate in the case of approved voluntary organisations or housing associations who provide a housing service for 'disadvantaged' persons. A simplification of the scheme which is currently in the legal form of a mortgage loan with fully subsidised repayments to a straight grant would reduce ongoing administrative commitments and perhaps help organisations seeking funds for the remaining 20% of the cost through borrowing on the security of the house properties.

The Department has also specified technical standards for the housing provided using the scheme of capital assistance which are based mainly on self-contained dwelling units built for elderly persons, whereas the scheme is intended to assist the housing of a number of other categories with different design needs and costing requirements.

The emphasis on fully equipped self-contained dwelling units in the technical standards may not be appropriate to the needs of the frail elderly, handicapped or homeless persons who would require more communal support facilities for assisted independent living in a sheltered housing service. The Department has indicated that a degree of flexibility is allowed in this regard.

On the other hand, the limit of £20,000 on the assistance available per unit is not adequate to meet the cost of the larger accommodation required for a family such as single parents with children of different sexes over the age of ten years.

The problems which face social housing organisations in dealing with ongoing running costs such as maintenance, management and social supports have not yet been dealt with adequately.

Section 12 of the 1966 Housing Act did provide for 'periodic contributions' to approved social housing organisations, but with no current defined scheme of assistance this power has contributed little to the development of social housing to date.

*Department of Environment Circular H5/84 as amended by Circular BC 9/85 gives details of the capital loan and subsidy scheme for approved organisations. Copies are available from the Department or The Housing Centre which functions as an advisory body for new housing associations or voluntary organisations wishing to develop a housing service.

The Health Boards do also have powers to assist with the cost of welfare and related services and have provided grants to voluntary organisations involved in running hostels and night shelters. But there is no defined scheme of assistance and, therefore, grants are largely paid on an ad-hoc basis, depending on the interest of the Health Board and the case made by the voluntary organisations. Without on going charitable donations, such voluntary housing/hostel services as do exist could not survive.

It is clear that for social housing organised by non-profit/voluntary organisations to reach its full potential, an integrated and defined scheme of assistance involving co-ordination between the Departments of Health and the Environment and the local statutory bodies is needed.

Local Statutory Bodies

Health boards, for example the Eastern Health Board, are anxious to encourage innovative social housing services provided by housing associations as a means to strengthen the community care approach to the needs of the elderly, the handicapped, homeless persons and the socially vulnerable.

By contrast, the larger local authorities have been mainly concerned with the development, organisation and financing of their own housing programmes. At senior management level they have not yet worked out any real policy to actively encourage, assist and enter into practical arrangements with non-profit, co-operative or voluntary housing organisations as part of an integrated approach to housing needs.

Similar problems in Britain, which together with Ireland, has one of the largest public/local authority housing sectors in Europe, resulted in the extension of the role of a State agency, The Housing Corporation, in 1974, to assist housing associations financially, to promote the work of housing associations, co-ordinate development plans for the social/voluntary housing movement, carry on liaison with the movement's own Federation, supervise management standards and, more recently, engage in new types of tenure arrangements. These housing associations now comprise some 2,700 in number and manage some 500,000 dwellings.

In Northern Ireland, the rapid expansion of the voluntary housing movement since 1979 has been funded by way of direct allocations for approved projects by the Northern Ireland Department of the Environment, working in close collaboration with the Northern Ireland Federation of Housing Associations.

An agency such as The Housing Corporation may not be necessary in a small country like Ireland but there is little doubt that the development of non-profit and voluntary housing here needs more priority attention by the managers of the large local authorities. If this cannot be achieved, serious consideration should be given to alternative arrangements to ensure adequate assistance and support.

Revamping Social Housing Policy Supports

On 19 September 1986, the Minister for the Environment stated that the current capital loan and subsidy scheme for the provision of rental housing for disadvantaged persons by approved non-profit and voluntary organisations will be 'revamped'.

The Housing (Miscellaneous Provisions) Bill, 1985 repeals Section 12 of the Housing Act, 1966 and replaces it with a new Section 5 which includes for the first time the power to pay a grant to approved bodies for housing purposes. In addition, the Bill provides for arrangements between local authorities and 'approved bodies' (e.g., co-operative or voluntary organisations and housing associations) for housing homeless persons.

However, improvements and simplifications of the 1984 scheme are needed along with increased capital allocations to take account of the number of organisations seeking to draw on funds for projects, especially in the £300,000 to £500,000 range. Indeed, capital requirements in excess of £500,000 are indicated for some projects which are already envisaged.

There is also concern that the proportion of new projects being developed is strongly in favour of housing the elderly and handicapped while other categories such as the homeless and socially vulnerable, single parent families, etc., who need this type of housing are not receiving as much attention. This is because it is harder to obtain charitable funds for this purpose and the lack of suitable sites in Dublin where the greatest need exists.

Organisations involved in trying to develop innovative housing services to cater specifically for marginal groups, or trying to develop mixed schemes, are inhibited by the limitations of the current scheme. These limitations apply to the overall financial assistance available and the technical standards which are linked to the maximum payment of £20,000 per dwelling unit.

The Housing Centre has made detailed Submissions to the Department of the Environment on aspects of the 80% Scheme of Assistance including the need to increase the overall capital allocation to fund projects (January 1987).

Examples of Projects Under Way

Some innovative new housing services have been planned or are under way by housing associations, mainly in Dublin in the context of the International Year of Shelter for the Homeless (IYSH) 1987. Examples of these are as follows:

1. Conversion of a house on South Circular Road to six dwelling units and communal space for homeless and socially vulnerable persons such as those who have left hospital. This has an anticipated cost of £160,000. (HAIL – the Housing Association for Integrated Living Ltd.)
2. Development of a non-profit rental housing scheme at Bonnybrook catering for families, single parents, handicapped persons, homeless and socially vulnerable persons in conjunction with local community groups on a site offered by the Catholic Church Diocese. The anticipated cost is £480,000 for approximately eighteen dwellings. (NABCo – The Co-operative Housing Association).
3. Rehabilitation and conversion of an inner city house for young single persons.

About £87,000 will be required. The project also includes an employment creation dimension for unemployed persons (NABCo – the Co-operative Housing Association).

4. Focus Point project catering for young single homeless persons: allocation of suitable premises/site by Dublin Corporation (Arran Quay).

5. Provision of night shelter/reception service with associated facilities at Ushers Island by Dublin Simon for homeless persons. This will include a housing service.

Conclusions — the Dimensions of an Enlarged Housing Policy

There is a need for Irish housing policy to take on board the concept of providing adequate capital assistance to facilitate the development of a social housing 'third arm' catering for a range of income groups for whom public housing or private home-ownership in the suburbs is not an appropriate solution. The potential for using a mixture of public funds and funds from the private mortgage agencies such as Building Societies and other financial institutions should be examined more intensively.

This would involve the development of a housing stock which is organised and managed to meet perceived needs between the public housing and private home-ownership sectors, to overcome the loss of the unfurnished private rental sector and to contribute to urban housing renewal.

Such an approach would recognise the value of decentralised housing management and maintenance as a means to facilitate security of tenure in group housing/apartments/flats, in newly built or converted housing, as a key part of an urban housing policy. This would involve a recognition of the value of actively encouraging the co-operative ownership and management of housing.

The contribution which voluntary organisations and housing associations can make in providing sheltered housing with support services for assisted independent living to meet the special needs of the elderly, the handicapped, socially vulnerable and homeless persons should be fully recognised as a valuable resource for integrating flexible housing management with social welfare support systems at local level.

The current pre-condition for active involvement by voluntary organisations and housing associations in the development of housing services, which is that they must first get large charitable contributions, should be reviewed so as to ensure that their participation, energy and interest is not lost because of financial limitations. This would involve the provision of a more realistic and complete package of financial assistance for this purpose than is available at present.

The application of the powers for development of the housing system envisaged in the Housing (Miscellaneous Provisions) Bill, 1985 should be fully explored so as to ensure that a range of schemes is set in place to give realistic support to the social housing movement and to enable it to reach its full potential in Ireland.

124

References

Baker, T. J. and O'Brien, L. M., *The Irish Housing System: A Critical Overview,* The Economic and Social Research Institute, 1979, Dublin.

Department of Health, *The Psychiatric Services: Planning for the Future,* Stationery Office, 1984, Dublin.

National Council for the Aged, *Housing of the Elderly in Ireland,* National Council for the Aged, 1985, Dublin.

CHAPTER 14

The future of the private rented sector: revitalisation or decay?

Cormac Ó Dúlacháin

The main disadvantages of the private rented sector are the quality of accommodation, the security of tenure and the actual cost relative to income.

Introduction

In 1982 Threshold published a report on private rented accommodation. The title chosen for that report was *Private Rented: The Forgotten Sector* (O'Brien *et al*, 1982). Today, five years later, private rented accommodation is more the ignored than the forgotten sector. Events in the last five years have concentrated the attention of communications media on this sector of accommodation, and various groups working with the disadvantaged have become more conscious of the problems which face many tenants. Threshold's Housing Advice Centres have continued to try and meet the problems in this sector on a daily basis with well over 2,000 cases per year. This chapter examines the future of the private rented sector, one that has been in a continuous if not rapid decay for many years. It examines whether there is a positive role in housing provision for private rented accommodation and, if so, how such a revitalisation can begin.

The Irish Position

Irish housing policy has concentrated on the provision of local authority housing for those in need and the encouragement of home ownership where at all possible.

Local authority housing was needed for two reasons: firstly, to make available accommodation with basic healthy facilities and adequate rooms for the occupants; and secondly, to provide this at a rent which the occupants could afford.

Most of those housed came from slums, many of which were in private ownership, so that from the earliest days private rented accommodation was seen as something from which people had to be rescued. This policy has been successful to the extent that significant numbers of people were rehoused. Infant mortality rates dropped as did the incidence of infectious diseases and, with the economic growth of the 1960s, many people went on to purchase their own homes, some with considerable State assistance.

The association of appalling living conditions with private renting, and the further historical connotation of the term 'landlord' in Ireland, has resulted in private renting being shunned. However, there is a difference between saying that further private renting on any large scale should be discouraged and saying there should be no private renting at all. Threshold's concern is to see whether in fact a small private rented sector can have an important role to play in a national housing strategy.

Debates about private renting can become irrational in that it is one area of life where there can be a direct conflict between private ownership and a person's housing need.

However, this should be balanced by a realisation that other housing sectors make a considerable use of private resources to the benefit of private owners, i.e., in the purchase of land for local authority housing, in the use of private contractors to build that housing, and in borrowing money to finance these activities. However, in the latter examples, the private benefit is so far removed from the end users as not to be seen.

Therefore, private renting should not be dismissed simply because there is an

128

*The **advantage** of the private rented sector is that the areas tend not to be stigmatised and are well serviced by public transport, shops, parks, libraries and public houses.*

element of private profit or benefit involved. What is of importance is the location, cost, quality and tenure arrangements as they affect tenants and whether it is cost effective for the State to encourage a limited level of private renting.

Private Rented Tenants

Private rented tenants do not form a cohesive group. Some have long term secure tenancies, some do not; some are short term or transitional users of the sector, others are either intentionally or unintentionally long term users. Some are poor or of limited resources, others are not; some are students or workers or unemployed, others are pensioners. Not all have the same needs or the same expectations. In the past few years, the supply of accommodation for those with employment has improved, with good quality accommodation available for rent in the suburbs at a cost which three or four working people would not find burdensome to share.

On the other hand, the economic recession and the rise in unemployment has meant that more flats and bedsits are now available for marginal groups, such as unemployment and single parents, than would have been available in the 1970s, when the demand from people coming to work in the city was greater.

The Advantages of the Private Rented Sector

One advantage of the private rented sector is its accessibility. There are no

129

waiting lists or points systems. Entry is available relatively easily. It is simply a question of having a comparatively small amount of money, e.g. £100.00 can cover a deposit and rent for a few weeks.

The other advantages relate to location and choice in that the areas tend not to be stigmatised – by contrast with much of local authority housing – and are well serviced by public transport, shops, parks, libraries and pubs. Traditional flatland offers a social mix of employed and unemployed, the married and the single. In that sense its location proves attractive. In many cases, the young unemployed would probably prefer to live there than in local authority accommodation that is probably of a better structural standard. Indeed, a significant factor among a cross-section of Threshold clients, from the young to the old, is their desire to live in the area in which they are currently renting while at the same time seeking better physical conditions, more security of tenure and some assistance with the cost of renting.

The Disadvantages of the Private Rented Sector

The disadvantages of the private rented sector affect the most vulnerable groups and individuals. The main disadvantages are the quality of the accommodation, the security of tenure and the actual cost relative to income.

In relation to the quality of the accommodation the problems vary from property to property but the common complaints are dampness, draughts, poor heating and ventilation, sharing of bathroom and toilet facilities, badly maintained common facilities, exposure to fire hazards, poor protection from theft, cramped bedsits, poor electrical wiring and fittings, furnishings of poor quality. These complaints do not relate to all properties but they are common and most common in the bottom end of the market where the socially vulnerable seek accommodation.

The problems that stem from lack of security of tenure centre on the relative ease with which a tenancy can be ended. This undermines the tenant's freedom to raise or complain about dissatisfactions they may experience. The short period of notice required and the difficulty in having deposits returned are also destabilising factors. These disadvantages tend to make the poorer a less mobile tenant, dependent on the landlord's whims, and can lead to a psychological subservience.

It is the issue of the cost, i.e., rent, that at times receives the greatest amount of attention, the complaint being that it is excessive or indeed extortionist given the facilities offered. In fact, with the decline in property values in recent years there has been little increase in rent costs in real terms. If one tries to analyse 'a reasonable rent', the question arises of the return on investment for the landlord.

Because of the low levels of local authority rents, there is little real public understanding of the costs involved in the management, maintenance and repair of property.

It would be wrong to assume that a property audit would indicate that rents should be lower. Rents tend to be more related to the overall market situation, in terms of the purchasing power of tenants and the availability of accommodation, as opposed to being set by a property-by-property assessment. What needs to be done is somehow to assess what a 'reasonable landlord' who manages and maintains his property fairly should expect. The more demands there are in terms of standards of repairs and services and security of tenure, the more the issue of cost looms. This whole issue again indicates how the cost factors which are hidden in the public sector are more to the fore in the private landlord/tenant relationship.

In relation to rental costs, the real issue is the lack of support for tenants whose incomes are low. Private tenants are the least subsidised. The subsidies which do exist are restrictive. Thus, for the growing numbers of poor or unemployed people living in 'flatland', the fear of defaulting on the rent and its consequences are very real.

The distinct advantage of the private rented sector is accommodation with ease of access, available to many different people, in reasonable locations and currently offering accommodation to a substantial number of vulnerable people.

A caveat has to be entered here – the current reasonable availability of accommodation could be a temporary factor. An upswing in the economy could see the single parent, the elderly person, the family with children and the unemployed becoming unwelcome tenants again.

In the last few years, there has been a noticeable trend whereby houses that were in flats have been sold and converted to family homes. This raises the question of whether there will be a shortage of accommodation in the private rented sector in the 1990s. If we accept the advantages of the sector, especially the social mix which it achieves and the flexibility which it provides, then we must address the issue of repairs and conditions of tenure. If this is not done, and if the private sector further declines in terms of volume, then these properties will revert to either commercial or private use and a further polarization of society will take place because the local authorities cannot afford to acquire or provide substantial accommodation in the areas where private letting is prominent. Indeed private renting may have a role in revitalising our city centres.

The main argument against any control or regulation of private rented accommodation is that it is counter-productive in that it discourages people from letting accommodation and discourages maintenance of dwellings. This reduces the supply of dwellings which thereby results in higher rents, as rents in this sector depend on the balance of supply against demand.

The counter argument is that when the demand for the market is in *decline* – as it is at present – this is then the right time to clean up and improve the sector, especially when building and improvement works may be cheaper in real terms than heretofore. Standards and regulations are part of everyday commercial activity and even more so when the consumer is a member of the public. We do not hesitate to control the production of food products, so why should we shy away from setting numerous safety and health regulations for accommodation? If such regulations scare people out of the market then it opens up the possibility for housing associations to be actively promoted and the possibility of their acquiring property being vacated by private landlords at a price that reflects its real housing value as opposed to the speculative values of the 1970s. This can only happen if housing associations are actually in place and have access to resources and incentives as proposed in Chapter 13. If this opportunity is not seized upon over the coming years, then areas like Ranelagh and Rathgar will revert to upper class areas and private rented tenants will have to turn in greater numbers to local authorities whose resources and accommodation options will be limited.

Housing Associations

The development of housing associations could provide a satisfactory form of ownership and management, with tenants being co-owners rather than being subservient to landlords. However, there is no magical formula to affordable housing. The cost of acquiring or building a property is only the start.

Therefore, a housing association, to live up to its future responsibilites in terms of repairs and renewals, may have to charge a rent related to, if not more than, the current market rent. The return from this would be in the form of decent secure accommodation offering a flexibility in housing resources at a time when there is increasing concern at the polarization of the community as a result of housing policies. There is a need for some form of tenure between absolute home ownership and the costly State-sponsored local authority housing.

The Options

The option is to develop the private rented sector by promoting private landlords or housing associations or both. Threshold's option is to favour the development of housing associations by a special package of incentives reflecting the priority. The word 'landlordism' should not instinctively produce a dismissal as it is possible along with housing associations to have a controlled and regulated market in the provision of accommodation. This requires for a start a minimum level of regulation, which can be achieved by order of the Minister of the Environment. It is a matter for the State to decide what form of investment is warranted.

Past incentives for the construction industry, such as Section 23 of the 1981 Finance Act, have had the effect of providing exclusive luxury rented accommodation at the upper end of the market. What has been lacking is any incentive to provide rented housing for marginal groups.

In comparative terms, private rented tenants obtain less Government support than other tenure groups. In many cases, tenants receive no support at all, no grant, allowances or tax relief; they receive less than that given to home owners and less than that given to local authority tenants.

There are some rent allowances, paid mainly to tenants of former rent controlled dwellings and to tenants in receipt of Supplementary Welfare. The Commission on Social Welfare in 1986 proposed the introduction of a statutory based housing benefit. While such a system would have the advantage of achieving an equitable contribution to the housing costs of all citizens, it needs to be carefully thought out. Any housing benefit paid in the private rented sector should have a progressive element – it should be concerned in some way with achieving an improvement in housing and tenure conditions and not merely in subsidising housing costs.

It is clear that legislation at present provides for the orderly phasing out of secure former rent controlled tenancies as tenants die. The only secure form of tenancy that can currently be obtained is that under the 1980 Landlord and Tenant Act where a tenant of twenty years has a right to a thirty year lease.

Few of the tenants with whom Threshold is concerned manage to stay or indeed want to stay twenty years in the one flat or bedsit. Yet there are quite a number of tenants who have been many years moving from flat to flat, never really enjoying any form of security or developing a sense of belonging. Many middle-aged and elderly people are slow to approach local authorities for assistance, and this is especially true of those who are single. It is this continuous lack of long term security that contributes to the tenant's dependancy on the landlord.

The Future

It is possible to achieve an improvement in living standards for many people without necessarily having to involve the full costs associated with local authority housing provision. The physical resource in terms of houses exists; it is a question how best to turn it to beneficial use. While it is in many ways an issue for the big cities with their high concentration of accommodation, at the same time each market town has its own small private rented sector.

Local authorities are only too well aware that, in the past, private rented accommodation was seen as a route to a local authority house, the poor conditions attracting higher points. The competition for points precipitated an endurance test as to who could suffer most in order to obtain priority for rehousing. Today the huge backlog of housing needs has been taken care of and we are now concerned with meeting current needs as they arise.

As it stands, private rented accommodation is one continuous source of problems. We must either accept a broader housing role for local authorities and the resultant costs, or we must try different strategies.

Over the last eight years, Threshold has intervened in many disputes. The very nature of the landlord and tenant relationship gives rise to disputes and not all are one sided. A side effect of the distaste for landlordism in Ireland is lack of regard for people's obligations as tenants. Not all these disputes will be resolved by changes in policy or legislation. What is needed is to pilot a more formal conciliation service through which Threshold, on the basis of agreed standard terms of tenancies, would try to resolve disputes.

In summary, the priority areas for action in the private rented sector are as follows. First, there is a need to seek an improvement in physical conditions by means of both setting minimum standards and extending housing improvement grants to effectively cover houses in multi-occupation. Second, we need to legislate for securer tenancy arrangements. Third, we must link any housing benefits or rent allowances to a form of progressive improvement of housing and tenure conditions. Fourth, we need to encourage through special incentives the development of housing associations to provide for (a) special needs groups, and (b) people who voluntarily wish to be part of a co-operative rent group or for whom owner occupation is too expensive or is not necessary. Finally, the establishment of a formal Landlord and Tenant Conciliation Scheme must be supported.

Reference
O'Brien L., and Dillon, B., *Private Rented: the Forgotten Sector,* Threshold, 1982, Dublin.

CHAPTER 15

The history and future of the Housing (Miscellaneous Provisions) Bill 1985

Dick Shannon

Introduction

The Housing (Miscellaneous Provisions) Bill, 1985, was published on 17 October 1985. It passed the second stage in Dáil Éireann on 4 November 1986, but lapsed with the dissolution of the 24th Dáil in January 1987.

The main purposes of the Bill are:
1. To revise and update the statutory framework for the provision, management and letting of local authority housing so as to ensure, in particular, that the needs of persons such as the homeless, the aged, the disabled, travellers, etc. get due priority in the formation and the allocation of dwellings.
2. To entrust to housing authorities additional responsibilities and powers in regard to the accommodation of homeless persons.

The Bill also provides statutory backing for a number of schemes of grants and subsidies which were introduced in recent years and certain sections of it provide for technical amendments of existing housing or other legislation.

In so far as it relates to homeless and marginal people, the Bill, despite some fundamental defects, is the most significant and progressive housing measure since the passing of the Housing Act, 1966.

While the main concern of the 1966 Act is the relief of overcrowding and bad housing conditions, the priority of the 1985 Bill is to ensure that certain categories of persons such as the homeless have access to suitable housing. The Bill is undoubtedly the first serious attempt by Government to formulate a policy on the housing needs of homeless people.

The History of the Bill

The history of the Bill is the history of Government neglect of the problems and needs of the homeless. A decade ago, the Parliamentary Secretary to the Minister for Social Welfare, Mr Frank Cluskey TD, in an address to the Annual General Meeting of the Dublin Shelter for Men conceded: "In welfare provisions throughout the years there has tended to be a neglect of the problems of homeless people" *(The Irish Times,* 8 December 1976). While Government neglect manifested itself in nearly every issue relating to the homeless, it was particularly blatant in the area of accommodation. Widespread confusion reigned for years over which State body, health board or local authority, had statutory responsibility for providing accommodation for the homeless. This confusion resulted in homeless people being shunted from health board to local authority and vice versa.

The Health Act, 1953

Under Section 54 of the Health Act, 1953, health authorities are obliged to provide institutional assistance to those unable to provide shelter for themselves. Shelter and maintenance were to be provided in county homes or similiar institutions run by the health authority.

In 1968 an Inter-Departmental Report recommended a change of role for the county home (Inter-Departmental Committee on the Care of the Aged, 1968).

136

While admitting that casuals were a social problem, the Report stated: "the committee did not regard it as necessary to make recommendations in regard to casuals." As a result of the Report, the role of county homes changed significantly, with many being closed down and others being redesignated.

A survey, carried out on behalf of the Simon Community in 1982, showed that 53% of county homes had closed or had reduced their provisions for homeless people. Another interesting finding of the survey was when asked "Are you, to your knowledge, under any statutory obligation to provide accommodation for the single homeless?", five county homes said 'no,' five said 'yes' and three 'did not know' (Doherty, 1982).

This lack of consensus among county homes as to their role and function in relation to the homeless was reflected in the comments of the most senior health board officials.

In 1977, the Chief Executive Officer of the Mid-Western Health Board was quoted as saying that the Health Board had a statutory obligation to cater for the homeless (*The Irish Times*, 2 April 1977). The Chief Executive Officer of the North-Eastern Health Board commented in 1978 that the Board "only had a function in relation to genuine mendicants" (*Drogheda Independent*, 20 January 1978), while in 1980 the Chief Executive Officer of the South-Eastern Health Board stated that "the obligation on the Health Board was more traditional than legal" (O'Brien, 1981).

The Housing Act 1966

Any 'able bodied' single homeless person seeking accommodation under the Housing Act, 1966, was likely to be disappointed in most parts of the country. The 1966 Act is concerned with the relief of overcrowding and bad housing conditions, and Section 60 obliges local authorities to adopt a scheme of priorities for that purpose. The scheme must aim to provide suitable housing for people who, in the local authority's opinion, are in need of housing and are unable to provide it from their own resources. Preference may be given outside the scheme of priorities to certain categories of people such as the disabled and the elderly. A single homeless person, who is not elderly or disabled, to be eligible for permanent accommodation must apply for housing, be accepted as being in need of accommodation, and qualify for housing on the basis of priority laid down in the local authority's scheme of letting priorities.

In determining priorities, factors such as overcrowding, lack of toilet facilities etc., in present accommodation are taken into consideration, with the result that a single homeless person who has no accommodation at all has little chance of getting housing. In practice, present housing policy gives priority to families and the elderly.

Some local authorities are adamant that they have no responsibility at all in this area as is obvious from the following extract from a letter written by an Assistant County Manager to members of his Corporation:

The Corporation has not a prime responsibility in this matter; it is considered that the only possible further action that can be taken is to urge the . . . Health Board to provide the necessary accommodation (Simon Community, 1982).

The West Cork administrative division of Cork County Council has said:

This Department does not generally rehouse single able-bodied people. These people are expected to provide their own accommodation (Simon Community, 1984).

There are, however, some local authorities which are willing to consider single homeless people for housing. In a survey on local authority housing provision carried out by the Simon Community in 1983, six local authorities said that they accepted residents of hostels and shelters onto their housing lists (Simon Community, 1984).

Commenting on the lack of clarity in relation to statutory responsibility, the then Minister for State at the Department of the Environment, Mr Ruairi Quinn TD, said in 1983:

I want to turn to the perceived role of the local authorities under the 1966 Housing Act and the role of the Health Boards under the 1970 legislation. There seems to be, in varying parts of the country and among different people operating on both systems, a reluctance to clarify where one set of responsibilities begins and another ends. Administrators – with the best possible intentions – will adopt a position which they think protects their Minister's interest. But as a result, groups are neglected (Simon Community, 1983).

The Demand for Legislation

In the early 1980s the demand for Government action and legislation grew. In its submission to the Department of the Environment for its proposed White Paper on Housing Strategy for the 1980s, the Simon Community argued that a White Paper should include adequate reference to homelessness and concrete measures to protect and provide for the homeless and those vulnerable to homelessness (Simon Community, 1982). It should be noted that this White Paper never materialised.

The Government's continued inaction led Independent Senator Brendan Ryan to introduce a Homeless Persons Bill in Seanad Éireann in 1983, which had the effect of sharpening the debate on homelessness.

The Bill, which passed the second stage in the Seanad on July 18, 1985, defines homelessness and makes the local authority responsible for housing the homeless person. While the Government opposed the Bill, the then Minister for the Environment, Mr Ruairi Quinn TD, said during the debate on the second stage:

The case for the present Bill is based, to a large extent, on this perceived ambiguity of responsibility for the provision of accommodation for homeless persons. I support that Bill insofar as it highlights that case. I would accept that there is a need for clear, sharp guidelines as to the divisions of responsibility between Health Boards and housing authorities and for a better understanding by these bodies of their respective roles (*Parliamentary Debates*, Seanad Éireann, 9 November 1983, Col. 467).

The Minister went on to give an undertaking that the Government would introduce its own legislation.

Ad-Hoc Committee on Homelessness

Also in 1983, the Minister for Health set up an ad-hoc committee, comprising representatives of the Department of Health, the Department of Social Welfare, the Department of the Environment, the health boards and the local authorities, to investigate the respective responsibilities of the health boards and the local authorities in relation to the homeless.

The Ad-Hoc Committee received submissions from a number of organisations including The Housing Centre, the Simon Community and CentreCare. In its submission The Housing Centre recommended that the housing system rather than the health boards should provide suitable housing for the homeless; in relation to local authority housing it recommended that:

Specific provision should be made in waiting list regulations and local authority allocation methods to facilitate homeless single persons, backed up by new legislation to protect and assist the homeless (The Housing Centre, 1983).

CentreCare in its submission stated:

The primary concern of people of no fixed abode is accommodation. We feel that responsibility for accommodating the homeless should lie with the Department of Environment and the local authorities, with support from Health Boards where appropriate.

Recommending that the Department of the Environment and the local authorities be responsible for housing the homeless, the Simon Community in its submission pointed out:

that most homelessness is avoidable, given the appropriate economic and social policies . . . that most residents in hostels need not be there, given the provision of sensitive housing policies.

The Ad-Hoc Committee issued its report at the end of 1984. It recommended that:

1. Health Boards should be responsible for homeless persons who require special care and who would not be capable of independent living.
2. Housing Authorities should be responsible for persons who are currently residing in hostels and who are capable of living in and want independent accommodation.

The Committee said it "recognised that the recommendations in this report, particularly those in relation to the responsibilities of housing authorities, can only be fully implemented under a legislative framework which permits a redirection of priorities within the housing authority programme" (The Housing Centre, 1985).

As a result of the Report of the Ad-Hoc Committee, the Department of Environment introduced an arrangement whereby there would be liaison between local authorities and health boards. According to the then Minister for the Environment, Mr. Liam Kavanagh TD, this arrangement should be such "as to ensure that one or other of those bodies would accept responsibility for each individual homeless person coming to their attention or that a person is referred from one to the other only with prior agreement" *(Parliamentary Debates,* Dáil Éireann, 3 December 1985, Col. 978).

Developments in Official Policy

The year 1984 saw a small but significant change in official policy towards the homeless. The Department of Environment announced a new financial aid scheme (Circular H5/84 of 22 March 1984) under Section 12 of the Housing Act, 1966, to assist the provision of housing accommodation for elderly and other disadvantaged persons by non-profit and voluntary organisations. The scheme provided loan finance and a subsidy towards loan charges for the provision of accommodation by approved bodies for certain categories of housing need. The certain categories include homeless persons.

There was also a change in the housing policy of Dublin Corporation. The problems that homeless people had in obtaining local authority housing were outlined to a special meeting of the Corporation in January 1984. As a result, the Corporation decided in principle to allocate fifty flats of medium and high demand specifically for homeless people at various locations around the city.

Support for Legislation

The campaign by voluntary groups for legislation received valuable support from a number of official reports published in recent years. The National Planning Board recommended that "responsibility for the housing of homeless people should be transferred from the Department of Health to the local authorities who should work closely with voluntary agencies and with community welfare agencies in developing appropriate programmes to tackle this problem" (National Planning Board, 1984, p.285).

The National Youth Policy Committee recommended that: "Legislation be enacted to place a statutory responsibility on some public authority for making provision for homeless young people" (National Youth Policy Committee, 1984, p. 156). The Committee of Inquiry into the Penal System had this to say: "There is clearly a need for the state and other public authorities to reconsider their policy towards, and their provision for, the homeless in general" (Committee of Inquiry into the Irish Penal System, 1985, p.34).

It was the cogent arguments advanced in reports and submissions by voluntary organisations and their persistent demands for legislative action, together with Senator Brendan Ryan's Bill, which helped to effect a dramatic change in the official perception of homeless people. And with this change of perception there gradually emerged a Government policy on the housing and accommodation needs of the homeless and marginal groups which was embodied in the Housing (Miscellaneous Provisions) Bill, 1985.

The Future

The Bill represents real progress in that it is a recognition by Government that homelessness is essentially a housing problem. The Bill has many positive features:

1. It attempts to define homelessness (Section 2).

2. It clearly extends the responsibility of the housing authorities to cater for the homeless (Section 10).

3. It provides that housing authorities specifically include homeless persons in the estimates of the housing requirements of their area (Section 8).

4. It provides that housing authorities, in addition to revising the code for dealing with unfit and overcrowded housing and involuntary sharing, shall be obliged to make an annual assessment of the need for provision by the authorities of adequate and suitable housing accommodation for homeless persons, travellers, disabled persons and the elderly. Housing authorities must give notice of the making of the annual assessment to certain other housing authorities, health boards, voluntary organisations and other bodies (Section 9).

5. It provides the legal framework for the payment of loans, subsidies and grants by local authorities to approved non-profit and voluntary associations involved in the provision of rented housing for disadvantaged persons (Sections 5 and 23).

However, the Bill contains some fundamental defects which undoubtedly will have the effect of excluding from its scope a large number of homeless people.

Definition of Homeless

The definition of homelessness contained in Section 2 is far too narrow and exclusive. It does not include:
– people living in hostels
– Travellers
– those who have accommodation but are forced to leave because of violence from some other person residing in it.

'Intentionally Homeless'

The Section 2 definition includes a limiting provision relating to 'intentional' homelessness. The housing authority has only to be of the opinion that a person is responsible for his or her homelessness and he or she is outside the scope of the legislation. This section is pernicious, socially judgemental and a throwback to the Poor Law era. Its interpretation will lead inevitably to variations in policy and practice by housing authorities. It is essentially a loophole, an escape clause for some housing authorities to evade their responsibilities.

Annual Assessment

The listing of specific categories of persons in Section 9 to which housing

141

authorities must have regard in preparing an annual assessment does not include one of the most vulnerable groups, that is, young people leaving institutional care or without family accommodation.

The Duty on Housing Authorities

The duty imposed on the housing authority in Section 10 is too vague and imprecise. The only duty expressly placed on the housing authority is to "take such steps as they consider appropriate to ensure that suitable accommodation is made available for occupation" by the homeless person. From the wording it would appear that it is not mandatory for the housing authority itself to provide accommodation.

Second, Section 10(2) empowers a housing authority to arrange lodgings or to contribute to the cost of such accommodation or lodgings. There is no provision for safeguards to ensure that homeless people do not end up in accommodation of poor standard, overcrowded bed-sits etc.

Third, Section 10(3) provides that a housing authority may specify a period for which accommodation is made available. This would seem to give the housing authority a wide power to terminate the accommodation provided and could considerably undermine the homeless person's security of tenure.

Independent Living

The duty of a housing authority applies to a person who is "capable of living independently". This qualification owes its origin to the Report of the Ad Hoc Committee on Homelessness. The Committee in drawing up guidelines for local authorities and health boards made a distinction between homeless persons who require special care who would not be capable of independent living and other homeless people.

The concept of 'independent living' is a palpable absurdity, sociologically unsound and not easily susceptible to objective evaluation. It ignores the fact that very few people in society, with the possible exception of a handful of hermits, are truly capable of independent living. Furthermore, it appears to contradict the trend towards sheltered and special needs housing which is being provided by local authorities, housing associations and voluntary organisations with assistance from the Department of the Environment.

Funding

The Bill in its present form raises the issue of adequate funding for voluntary organisations working with the homeless. Section 10(2) empowers housing authorities to make arrangements for the provision of accommodation for homeless persons and to make a financial contribution towards the cost of the accommodation.

This section will have little value unless a defined scheme for funding such contributions is established. Experience shows that the powers conferred under Section 12 of the Housing Act, 1966, in relation to "periodic contributions" have proved to be largely worthless because of the absence of a specific funding arrangement. It should be noted that at present the financial assistance available to voluntary organisations operating hostels and shelters is based to a large extent on ad hoc grants, mainly from health boards. The lack of a proper funding arrangement at present means that voluntary organisations expend a lot of time and energy on fund-raising and the day-to-day struggle for survival.

Conclusion

The Housing (Miscellaneous Provisions) Bill, 1985, is a progressive measure. It clearly provides a statutory framework for housing provision in this country. It is obviously an attempt to come to terms with the issue of statutory responsibility for the homeless and to ensure that the most vulnerable in our society have access to housing.

However, unless the shortcomings outlined above are remedied, there is a danger that the eventual legislation will have no relevance for large sections of the homeless, and it will not be the comprehensive response to homelessness which was originally promised. Because of these major defects, reflecting perhaps a residual prejudice towards certain social groups, there is a real danger that the Bill will fail to have any impact on the lives of many homeless people and marginal groups.

It should be noted that the Bill when passed, in whatever form, will be enabling legislation. Its effectiveness and the manner in which it will be implemented will be very much determined by the regulations drawn up by the Minister and statutory instruments. And, needless to say, the legislation will have no chance at all if adequate funds are not made available by the Exchequer.

If, for any reason, a Bill is not enacted, the issue will not conveniently disappear. As a result of developments over the past few years, it is now official policy that there is an urgent need for legislation. Homelessness is on the political agenda and it will remain there. Legislation is inevitable. Voluntary bodies expect it, the homeless need it and justice demands it.

References

Committee of Inquiry into the Irish Penal System. *Report,* Stationery Office, 1985, Dublin.

Doherty, Vincent, *Closing Down the County Homes,* Simon Community (National Office) 1982, Dublin.

Inter-Departmental Committee on the Care of the Aged, *The Care of the Aged Report, 1968,* Stationery Office, 1980, Dublin.

National Planning Board, *Proposals for Plan 1984-87,* Stationery Office, 1984, Dublin.

National Youth Policy Committee, *Final Report,* Stationery Office, 1984, Dublin.

O'Brien, Justin, 'Poverty and Homelessness' in *One Million Poor?* edited by Stanislaus Kennedy, Turoe Press, 1981, Dublin.

Simon Community (National Office), *The Case for a Homeless Persons Act,* 1982, Dublin.

Simon Community (National Office), *Living on Fresh Air,* 1983, Dublin.

Simon Community (National Office), *Housing: An Agenda for Action,* 1982, Dublin.

Simon Community (National Office), *The Case for a Homeless Persons Act,* 4th Edition, 1984, Dublin.

The Housing Centre, *Social Housing,* No. 1, 1983, Dublin.

The Housing Centre, *Social Housing,* No. 7, 1985, Dublin.

CHAPTER 16

Housing and design

Philip Geoghegan

There are many redundant buildings throughout Ireland which could provide good housing accommodation whilst reinforcing the existing urban structures.

Introduction

This chapter outlines some key design issues at a broad, strategic scale in housing. Possible areas of intervention where design may be a critical factor in influencing policy decisions are covered. The chapter argues for efficient use and adaptation of existing built resources and of the housing stock as the most appropriate approach to provision for homeless persons and families.

Housing Quality and the Homeless

Quality in the housing environment – not only good houses to live in, but good neighbourhoods and a stimulating visual environment should be an attainable aspiration for the whole community. Unfortunately it is still a long way off. Poor quality, badly constructed and inadequately serviced housing and associated facilities continue to be prevalent, inescapably contributing to social tensions and breakdown.

Admittedly, the impact of poor housing areas on social behaviour is difficult to quantify. But this should not remove the issue from priority consideration, although all too often that seems to happen.

Ireland's building boom of the last twenty years has abruptly stopped. Throughout that period of huge expansion in Dublin, arguments for better community infrastructure, better housing design, a more balanced housing mix, a better dispersal of housing categories and better housing environments were responded to conscientiously, if only in part, by the local authorities and minimally, if at all, by the private sector. Ballymun, Darndale, Finglas at one stage were idealistic concepts for new communities which, with hindsight, were doomed to fail.

At present, if the homeless are to be housed at all, it is likely that they will end up being fitted into estates and areas which are difficult to let and which are already accommodating 'problem' families in problem environments.

Few of the homeless categories need special design provision. Certainly, old people and the handicapped need special internal provision. But for single people, single parents and divided families, housing requirements are neither less nor more than those of other people in need of housing, with space requirements, of course, being dependent on family size.

There is a critical shortage of small (one and two bedroomed) units available for social housing use. Almost all of this type of accommodation is in the private sector. The first question, then, is to establish whether larger, or different houses can be adapted for smaller unit use.

The other question of whether purpose-built hostels should be built is one of social policy, not of design. Insofar as the creation of institutions *is* an architectural issue I would feel that homeless people should be given accommodation which looks like and feels like anyone else's home, even though it may be larger or purpose built.

Currently, the provision of any kind of housing, whether public, private or voluntary, is under great pressure from cut-backs in public expenditure and declines in real income. It is unlikely that new building programmes will occur specifically for homeless categories, with the exception of Travelling people. Nevertheless, a sensitive reshuffle of priorities and a sympathetic financial structure could encourage a limited amount of new building and an intelligent adaptation of houses from the existing stock to alleviate the problems of homeless groups.

Housing Pre-1900

It is likely that most opportunities for the homeless people will arise in the adaptation of existing housing which was constructed before 1900.

There is a large stock of unimproved houses in every part of the country, located within towns and cities, which could be adapted for different occupation. Georgian and Victorian houses have proved to have flexible and adaptable plan-forms. There is considerable experience of such adaptation to high standards among Housing Associations in Britain and Northern Ireland; to a much lesser degree, in the Republic. There is also a great deal of experience in adaptation at a relatively low level – comprising short-life housing – where minimum repairs are made to make a house habitable without undertaking long-term major improvement works.

There is a minefield of requirements under planning and bye-laws and there are many pitfalls for the unwary voluntary group. Fire escape requirements may be very difficult and expensive to meet. The application of the building regulations to existing buildings is also a source of confusion and uncertainty. Despite these problems, the improvement of existing houses in the older areas of cities and towns remains an attractive proposition. The houses are in well-established communities and are generous in their space provision. Cost per square foot is likely to be less than for new units although cost per unit may be equivalent.

Post War Housing

Newer, and smaller, houses which were built after 1945 may also be used successfully. They are generally not easily adapted for self-contained units, but they have been used successfully as homes for single parents, sharing living, kitchen and bathroom facilities and occupying their own rooms.

Improvement of Large-Scale Housing Developments

An important element of city centre housing provisions exists in large blocks of flats, the earliest and best-known being the Iveagh Trust buildings in the Kevin Street and St Patrick's area of Dublin. Major rehabilitation programmes are necessary for these buildings and others under Corporation ownership to provide adequate up-to-date housing provision. Rehabilitation costs for full rehabilitation may be as expensive as smaller-scale new residential units, but as high-density residential areas in the city centre the effective improvement could provide much more than small scale new units would, as it could be instrumental in holding together the well-established city communities.

Such improvements need to be accompanied by environmental improvement works in order to upgrade the general appearance as well as the particular standards of the residential units. It is possible to consider lower-grade improvements with a net reduction in density but, in that case, interior space is used less effectively.

Housing Over Shops

A seemingly untapped source of accommodation, the unused and often derelict upper floors of shops and other commercial premises in Ireland's towns and cities represents an inadequately-studied potential. A preliminary study undertaken with the shopkeepers of Shandon Street in Cork, where 20% of upstairs premises were unused, indicated a willingness to respond to ideas for re-use of upper-floors, although there were problems concerned with the achievement of separate access, and there appeared to be no real financial incentive for shopkeepers to act. However, under different policy structures and possibly through the formation of Street or Area Trusts as undertaken by some universities in the UK, there would seem to be real potential for housing units for single people, couples and small families, and a positive contribution to urban regeneration.

Adaptation of Other Buildings

Successful and imaginative adaptation of warehouse and mill buildings in the UK (for example, in Glasgow) and the Netherlands for housing use has been achieved. A feasibility study in Carrick-on-Suir was carried out in 1982 for conversion of a small mill building which showed costs falling within the Department of the Environment's limits under the Housing Package. There are many redundant buildings of this type throughout Ireland in towns and villages which could provide good housing accommodation whilst reinforcing the existing urban structures.

Newly-built 'Purpose Built' Housing for Homeless Categories

Numerous housing schemes – though not enough – exist for old people throughout Ireland, built by local authorities and voluntary groups. Whilst they may form part of a wider structured community in smaller towns the groups tend to be small, maybe five or six units; in larger urban areas, sheltered housing may be twenty or thirty units in size. They have in common a single use, and they inevitably become identified as separate. It is a challenge to create balanced communities and to avoid ghettos or concentration. The dispersal of special categories within housing areas may be bureaucratically awkward but it is certainly socially desirable. The identification of certain areas for 'problem' families is undesirable as it is a self-fulfilling policy, guaranteeing the permanency of 'problem' estates.

In an idealised picture, it is both possible and desirable to disperse old people, single people, single parents, so that community support becomes locally based and implicit, the diversity of the grouping enriching everyone – like the village street.

The Bonnybrook project for twenty special-category houses is a pragmatic attempt to provide for diverse needs and to establish a balance with some hope of social interaction across generations and circumstances. The scheme is primarily for small households of one, two and three people, but it is hoped to house some larger families, a number of disabled, wheelchair people, single parents and old people. The scheme will have its own 'room-sized' social centre.

References

The Housing and Urban Design Research Unit, and University of Groningen (Dept. of Geography). "The Shandon Project", 1980, Dublin, mimeo.

O'Connor, D., *Housing in Dublin's Inner City,* 1977, Dublin.

CHAPTER 17

A Case Study in the Liberties of Dublin

Michael Mernagh

Some of the new housing in the Liberties of Dublin, overlooked by St Patrick's Cathedral.

Introduction

In Ireland over the years, there has been little or no opportunity or structures available for people to participate in decision making. People could not influence the manner in which decisions were implemented, even though in a number of cases their lives were adversely affected. Nowhere has this been more evident than in relation to physical planning and our capital city of Dublin. The past twenty years have witnessed the growing dereliction of our Inner City and the forced movement of large numbers of its young population to vast sprawling suburban estates many miles away from their relatives, kinship and social networks. The end result of this so-called 'development' is there for all to see in terms of alienation, loneliness and a host of social problems affecting both those who are left behind in the Inner City and those who find themselves in these new satellite towns. The physical blight of acre after acre of derelict sites, broken down buildings, decaying streets and flat complexes all contribute to a hostile and sometimes violent environment. What can local people and communities, who find themselves in this situation, do to stop the rot? The following is an account of what one such group of people have done and are continuing to do in order to have some say in shaping the future of their community and their environment.

The South Inner City Community Development Association

In early 1982 a small group of concerned people representing some local tenants associations came together to find some way of responding to the increasing neglect and deterioration of their community and their sense of powerlessness to do anything significant about it. Thus, the idea of the South Inner City Community Development Association (SICCDA) was born. The Association currently comprises all the major tenant, community and special interest groups in the Liberties (population c.12,000).

Aims of SICCDA

The following are its major aims:

– To promote and ensure, through community development, the total development of the area and its people in a manner acceptable to and suitably controlled by the people themselves.

– In conjunction with local people to design and initiate a programme which will cater for their social, economic, cultural and educational needs.

To achieve these aims the Association has embarked on an ambitious community development programme to cater for a variety of local needs It has initiated training and development projects dealing with youth, the elderly, homeless, families with special needs, including traveller families, the unemployed and with the general community environmental problems.

Profile of the Area and its People

The geographical area for the Association comprises the area of the oldest

152

community in Dublin known as the 'Liberties'. It covers approximately one square mile. It is an area whose history can be traced back to the Viking Settlement. It has experienced a rich influx of immigrant people bringing with them a wide range of crafts, trades and cultures.

It epitomises all that is good in the tradition and community values of Old Dublin and this sense of neighbourliness and friendliness is still very much in evidence.

The area, though very much alive in terms of its people, nevertheless exudes a certain air of physical decay, resulting in an environment which has become increasingly unhealthy and harsh.

The level of owner occupation of housing is 31.2% as against the national norm of 74%, with 35.3% of its dwellings in Dublin Corporation rented accommodation, and 31.5% of housing privately rented (source: Community survey by SICCDA carried out in 1982).

The area now has a youth (under twenty five) unemployment rate of 42.3% (source: Survey of Youth Needs carried out by SICCDA, 1985). Between 1976 and 1986, many thousands of jobs were lost in firms with household names. It is perceived by its population as having the twin ills of unemployment and danger from hard drugs affecting its young people.

It is in immediate need of playgrounds for its children and club facilities for its youth. Seventy six per cent of youth surveyed felt that they had too few or no facilities. Only 9.8% of its youth are involved in organised activities.

In this area, 90% of the youth feel that their prospects are now 'very bad' or 'terrible' and 57% felt that these same prospects will be worse in five years time.

In this area, only 0.7% of young people have a qualification from a third level institution. The youth receive little training in skills.

The area has an elderly population (sixty years of age and over) which is 19.5% of the total – twice the national average. Of these elderly people 52.6% live alone, and 60% are in bad health. Of the elderly, 56.1% are lonely and afraid, 35.6% have difficulty in going out and are therefore depressed and isolated, and 33.8% expressed a desire for small local neighbourhood centres where they could gather for recreational purposes.

In the area, 20% of all families were considered to be economically and socially deprived, and therefore were referred to social workers.

It is evident from the foregoing that the area is in need of urgent action in order to overcome the many problems which are outlined.

The Community Development Plan

The particular project which I wish to outline deals with the role of the community in the planning process. In a submission to An Taoiseach in December 1982 the Association highlighted aspects of what it saw to be the appalling physical blight, decay and environmental pollution which were destroying the community and creating a serious health hazard.

A number of specific recommendations were made, as follows:

- The need for a comprehensive survey of all public and privately-owned derelict sites and buildings as a first step towards community participation in the development of an integrated planning policy.
- The urgent need for more recreational, social and leisure facilities.
- The need for more adequate housing, in particular special housing for the elderly and the handicapped.
- The need to ensure the preservation of historic buildings.
- The need to curtail the heavy through traffic which was causing a serious environmental health hazard.

In pursuing these recommendations a special planning committee was established by the Association. This committee designed a phased programme of research and action.

Phase 1

Phase 1 of the work involved the following steps.

Surveys of Land Use

In November 1984, following a submission to the Minister for Environment, a grant was approved by the Inner City Group to finance a survey of buildings and sites in the Liberties area.

On foot of this grant the Association entered into contractual consultancy agreements with the School of Architecture, UCD to supervise and carry out the first phase of the project. It also involved six young local people under the Department of Labour 'Teamwork' scheme in this phase. The work began in March 1985.

Method of Work

Using the same survey techniques and ward reference numbers as the Planning Department of Dublin Corporation, a street survey of the area was undertaken between March 1985 and August 1985. The area covered is that as shown on ordnance maps (2363-6 to 25), covering about one square mile of the eastern part of the South Inner City.

In order to avoid duplication with the information on the land use maps of Dublin Corporation, it was agreed that the maps should show uses under the following categories:

Derelict: A building which has no roof or floors or a vacant site or a site used on a temporary basis or a site containing the remains of a structure or structures.

Disused: A building which has been blocked up or was unsuitable at the time of the survey.

Unused: A building which was for sale or temporarily not being used or to let.

154

Detailed information on each site and building and their uses, etc. is contained in extensive files held in the offices of the Association.

Major Findings

The survey revealed that there were 53.3 acres of land with derelict buildings on them or lands which had been cleared and were being used as car parks on a temporary basis in the area. There were also 8.6 acres of land possibly on their way to becoming derelict.

There were 227 acres of land occupied by buildings which were unused. In the latter two categories the areas indicated do not include the area of any building above the ground floor. These findings came as a shock even to those members of the Association who were aware of the physical blight in the area.

Phase 2

The aim of the second phase of the plan was that the needs of the Liberties Community:

1. be recorded and represented on a proposed Planning and Urban Design map of the area;

2. be presented to the Planning Department of Dublin Corporation for inclusion into the new Dublin Draft Development Plan.

In consultation with officials from the Planning Department of Dublin Corporation, it was agreed to reduce the study area to an agreed Central area which appeared, from the survey, to contain the most dereliction and correspondingly the greatest need for environmental action. The area covers 370 acres or 0.6 square miles.

Work Method

The project was located in a shop premises at 82 The Coombe, leased by SICCDA from Dublin Corporation. The purpose in choosing this location was that it was easily accessible to the public, thereby encouraging local people to drop in and discuss the ongoing work of the project.

In practice, the consultation process proved to be very democratic, with local neighbourhood associations and environmental groups consulting directly with the study team and the members of the planning committee of SICCDA.

Approximately thirty groups and individuals were consulted in all, over a period of ten weeks, by word of mouth, by circular letter and by direct contact with people. Some of these groups reported back to their neighbourhoods for further consultation. Views were sought on the levels of facilities and on the road widening proposals as outlined in the Dublin Corporation's draft development plan. The planning team having heard their views and needs, designed outline drawings to their satisfaction and matched their requirements to the possible site locations in their neighbourhoods.

The planning team, having heard and discussed the range of views and wishes,

155

assembled an outline map of these and brought them to the Central Committee of SICCDA for further discussion, clarification and approval.

When this process was over the completed plans were put on display at the Guinness Hop Store and representatives of the various Departments of Dublin Corporation were invited to view them and to discuss them with representatives of the Association. Following this, representatives of the Association entered into detailed discussions with officials from the Planning Department of Dublin Corporation.

Major Proposals

The main proposals can be summarised as follows.

Roads and Traffic

Without exception, everyone who was consulted objected to major road widening and motorway construction proposals for the area.

This opposition was not ill-considered or simply emotive, but was founded on the perception of the divisive impact of through-roads on the communities. The influx of car borne shoppers causes severe congestion, not only in the shopping streets, but also in the residential areas adjacent to the street. A number of proposals were made to alleviate this problem. One concerned the construction of three multi-storey car park buildings off the Coombe By-Pass, Thomas Street and Christchurch Place.

Housing

Everyone who was asked was of the opinion that greater resources should be invested in the construction of new housing in the area. Sites for such housing were identified in the plan. Sites at present suffering blight should be designated for housing redevelopment. The project identifies seven such sites on which 900 housing units could be built. Outline sketch designs for these are contained in the full report.

With a mix of local authority, co-operative and privately developed housing, the Liberties would see a regeneration of its falling population and the influx of a varied range of people committed to living in the Inner City.

Such influx would provide an adequate support base for existing schools and churches of the area so preventing their disuse and potential decay.

With regard to special needs housing, the Association stresses that in the proposed housing programme special attention should be paid to housing people such as the elderly, the handicapped, the homeless, and Travellers.

Neighbourhood Facilities

Many of the neighbourhood groups which were canvassed expressed a need for a meeting place or community centre adjacent to where they lived. Such centres, they felt, would give a much needed sense of identity to often anonymous flat blocks and provide an important community focus for the neighbourhood. It could, among other things, provide a day care facility for the elderly.

156

Community Facilities

There are few places, other than public houses, for young and old to meet. There is nowhere to which a family in distress may retreat or where a homeless or unemployed person may drop in for advice, counselling or skill training. There are no publicly available cultural centres, no library, no cinema, no theatre.

Briefs were formulated and sites identified for the establishment of a medical, family resource and day activity centre which would provide paramedical care and consultation services for the elderly, and workshops, coffee shops and counselling rooms for families in need and for rootless people. Such facilities could be allied to short stay accommodation or to sheltered housing for the elderly or other special needs group.

With such high levels of youth unemployment and corresponding activity in the area, the majority of those canvassed considered that the provision of a leisure centre, a sports hall and outdoor sports facilities were urgently required.

The only library in the area (Thomas Street) closed down some years ago. The project has identified the need for library facilities.

Urban Facilities

Because the Liberties incorporates and is adjacent to the historic medieval core of the city, it is considered essential that future development around the High Street area be of a type that exhibits aspects of the area's history, and provides a location for the artifacts discovered by the National Museum on the Wood Quay site. This could be an unequalled historical resource for Irish people and be a magnet for home-based and foreign tourists. The Liberties has high potential for tourist development and the establishment of a Heritage Centre allied to commercial and hotel development is proposed.

With the co-operation of An Taisce, 'landmark' buildings in the area have been identified and it is proposed that certain of these be considered and refurbished for cultural use.

The final and continuing phase of this project is to have these proposals implemented. The financial and the legal power to implement the proposals is beyond the resource and the control of communities such as the south inner city area.

Phase 3

Towards Implementation of the Plan

The plan is a community Development Plan in the full meaning of those terms. It is unlikely that the authorities have anything like such a comprehensive plan before them from any other source.

In formally proposing that this plan be incorporated into the Reviewed Development Plan, the planning committee of Dublin Corporation have taken the first step. The wishes and needs of people, including those most at risk in the community have been clearly identified and communicated to the relevant planners and decision-makers for their attention and action. The acid test of their commitment to real participation will be seen in their response.

Conclusions

The aim of the plan was to document the conditions of the area and to point to action needed. The plan shows the urgent need which exists to revitalise the Liberties area with new housing, new opportunities for jobs and improved facilities for community care, recreation and culture. In order that the aims be achieved there is need for commitment to action both by central Government and by local authorities.

There is now the opportunity to develop a new model of citizen participation in planning in Ireland. This has been a case study of a new type of planning, with public participation in the formulation of an area development plan and with the planning system taking account of everyday problems and needs and of the wishes of the community. In the past the wishes of those living in disadvantaged inner city locations have not been taken account of in the planning process.

With regard to the reactions of the community to the process of compiling the plan the following is a summary of a report from the planning team to the project team.

> The response we received from all parties consulted was one of openness and enthusiasm. The positive reactions we received were often tinged with mild expressions of disbelief that anything proposed by a Community Development Association, albeit assisted by the professional expertise available through a third level institution, would in fact be taken seriously by the powers that be.

> The fact that SICCDA and the team were receiving the full co-operation of the Planning Department of Dublin Corporation, helped in some way to diminish the often overwhelming sense of powerlessness experienced by those who see a system often operating against, rather than for, their interests.

> In the process of our consultation we found a high level of consensus concerning the problems and potential of the area. Those we spoke to, believed passionately in the future of their area and felt positive about what might happen if the political will was there to help them achieve their aims. (Gerry Cahill, Project Leader).

CHAPTER 18

Towards a settlement strategy

Stanislaus Kennedy/Justin O'Brien

Homeless people are particularly perceived as being different from the rest of the community: a common perception is that of a middle-aged group of people who have been living in hostels for years and sleeping rough. Terms such as vagrants, winos, alcoholics, dossers and bag ladies spring to people's minds. Being homeless is often seen as being one's own fault. It is caused by one's behaviour. A common perception is that homeless people do not want to change; that they are dirty, smelly, difficult or reclusive people.

People who become homeless are seen as a group apart, as being different from the rest of society. As such, they are seen as scarcely having the rights which are accepted as belonging to people in our society. Separate services have been provided for them: separate food, shelter and welfare services. Single homeless people do not have a right to a house and travellers do not have a right to a serviced site for a caravan. As homeless people are defined as being different, they are automatically excluded from participating in the rest of society, stigmatised and thus rendered powerless.

People who find themselves without a home do not fit the popular stereotype of the homeless person. Instead they are a heterogeneous group containing many sub-groups. Many are people who have fallen on hard times. But once they become homeless they gradually lose close ties with family and kinship. They tend to be poor, have inadequate income and are stigmatised. They tend never to describe themselves as 'homeless'.

Most people experience being out-of-home at some stage in their lives, but the vast majority of us are cushioned by relatives or friends. It is when those relationships break down and people disengage themselves from these ties that being out-of-home can extend for weeks, months and even years. It is generally these people who approach Focus Point for help. They have very special needs and special services are offered to them which enable them to move back into the mainstream of society and back into that community, rather than services which reinforce their exclusion.

In its effort to help people with special needs back into the community, Focus Point has developed a settlement strategy.

The Case for a Settlement Strategy

There are a number of reasons why a coherent settlement strategy is needed for people out-of-home. First, people who are out-of-home and have special needs require special forms of help. Prior to the establishment of Focus Point, this specialised help was not available in Dublin. Local Authorities see themselves as providing housing for people and not the type of settlement service required by many. Hostels provide accommodation for people out-of-home and have not sufficient financial resources to undertake a settlement service.

Second, the majority of people out-of-home want to be settled back into the community. Focus Point's experience shows that of the 889 people out-of-home in contact with the agency between September 1985 and September 1986, only 3% (26) actually wanted to live in hostel accommodation, while 97% (863) wanted to live in the community. This is also supported by the Focus Point survey on hostel residents in Dublin (February 1986) in which hostel staff stated that at least 38% of the existing hostel residents were capable of living in the community if they were given different types and degrees of support.

Third, there is a very high mobility of homeless people between Dublin hostels, as established by a Focus Point survey of February 1986. The study states that during the month of February 1986, 1,433 individuals were staying in Dublin hostels. During the same period 34% of this population moved: i.e. 488 moved in, out or between these hostels. The high mobility amongst hostel residents increases difficulties in helping people out-of-home to settle.

Ideally, there should exist an emergency or short-term hostel which immediately links people to a resettlement service which could provide them with suitable housing options and help them move from a state of homelessness back to a secure and suitable home of their own.

The Glasgow experience gives us a salutary lesson. In the early 1980s, 2,000 men and women were rehoused from hostels and lodging houses in Glasgow into mainstream tenancies. This experiment clearly showed that an effective settlement strategy can help to reintegrate people out-of-home back into the community. The Glasgow experience of settling single people from hostels is described at the end of this chapter.

An Ecology of Homelessness . . . An Ecology of Settlement

Focus Point has discovered an ecology of homelessness which identifies the stages through which a person can move into homelessness and through which a person can be helped to return home or to settle in another home of his/her own.

Not every person who is out-of-home necessarily goes through each of the four stages described here but it is Focus Point's experience that most people do go through some, at least, if not all, of these stages:

insecurity
crisis
transit
settlement

In this paper we now discuss these stages in relation to groups as they experience them.

Fig. 18.1 Stages of Being Out-of-Home

	LEAVING
	• A place/person that can help
	• Information
	OUT OF HOME
	• A person that can help
	• Information
	• Shelter
	• Food, clothing
	• Money
	LOOKING FOR A HOME
	• Advice counselling
	• Assessment of needs
	• Finding a suitable place
	• Stable income
	• Job planning
	• Support
	SETTLING AT HOME
	• Relationships
	• Security
	• Support
	• Activities
	• Secure income

Insecure Stage

This group represents people who have little or no security in their present home situation. They are people who are potentially homeless because of various factors in the home, e.g., violence, family break-up, a sudden death, change in income level, failure to find or loss of employment, threatened eviction.

Included in this group are those who migrate to Dublin or other cities in search of employment or who simply wish to live independently of their family. This is a normal process in our society and the majority of people manage to make this transition successfully. A minority do not. Their search for employment fails, and they are unable to secure accommodation. Particularly in cities, inadequate income often makes it impossible to secure accommodation.

Others include young unemployed people with little or no family contact. Some of these may return to their families at night but find themselves on the street for very long periods each day. Many of these young people are gradually drifting into the street culture and become vulnerable and at risk to drugs, prostitution and crime.

A significant number of these people suffer from physical and/or emotional abuse in the family, which leaves them in an insecure home. The particular reactions of these people to their problem will determine their route into homelessness. For example, some leave home and go to friends, others go to hostels, some leave home for short periods and then return, others may leave home for good.

Without sufficient income, information and support after leaving home, people quickly find themselves in a cycle of homelessness. As ties with family and friends weaken, they can easily become, through no fault of their own, disaffiliated and in a vicious cycle of homelessness and living on the fringes of society.

Focus Point's Response

Prior to a person leaving home, Focus Point can put forward alternative and possible solutions to a person's problem. For example, Focus Point can:

– Help people to obtain any necessary support, care or specialised assistance needed to remain in his/her present home.

– Help people make a smooth transition between their former and an alternative future home.

Fig. 18.2 Homelessness: Insecure Stage

Possible Needs	Focus Point Responses
Contact with a helping agency or individual	24 hour phone service
Accessible information	Information and advice service
Specialised help e.g. housing options, family intervention	Counselling skills
Referral to other agencies	Referral system
Support	Support

Between September 1985 and September 1986, 230 people who were threatened with homelessness and about to leave their home, contacted Focus Point.

163

Crisis Stage

The second group of people which Focus Point identifies are those who leave home because of a crisis. The crisis may be loss of job, separation, bereavement, family conflict, violence, illness, fire, discharge from an institution or a combination of these. Such events can leave a person or family with no place of their own. Homelessness can occur suddenly or as a result of personal trauma. Once the crisis occurs, choices are limited depending on a person's personal resources. Options include staying with other family members or friends, sleeping out, hostel care, bed and breakfast or hotel accommodation.

While a person's ability to return to their former home or community may have been threatened by such crisis, it may not necessarily be destroyed. The prospect of achieving this varies between individuals and families, depending on the factors which caused them to leave home in the first place, the personal trauma they have suffered and their own resources. Many of them can create a new home if given the necessary resources and personal support.

If the individual or family is not properly helped at this stage they are likely to remain homeless for a long period, possibly their whole lives.

Fig. 18.3. Homelessness: Crisis Stage

Possible Needs	Focus Point Response
Contact with a helping individual or agency	24 hour phone service and streetwork
Accessible information	Information on options, rights and entitlements
Emergency Accommodation	Referral to available emergency accommodation
Food	Low cost food
Money	Help obtaining social and supplementary welfare
Support	Support and follow-up

Focus Point Response

Once people become homeless, their immediate needs are: nutrition, shelter, information and support.

Between September 1985 and September 1986, 659 people who were in this crisis stage contacted Focus Point.

Transit Stage

Often homelessness is seen as a fixed state — a person who is out-of-home is described as homeless rather than a person who has *become* homeless due to circumstances.

Homelessness should be a transitionary stage rather than a fixed one and people, if they are forced out-of-home for any of a variety of reasons, should quickly be helped to return to a secure home of their own whether that be their former home or new accommodation.

Once people's basic needs have been met during the crisis stage, other needs may be addressed. These needs relate to securing more permanent housing and building a home of their own.

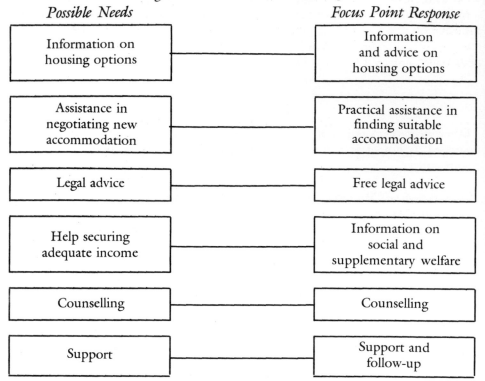

Fig. 18.4   Homelessness: Transit Stage

Possible Needs	Focus Point Response
Information on housing options	Information and advice on housing options
Assistance in negotiating new accommodation	Practical assistance in finding suitable accommodation
Legal advice	Free legal advice
Help securing adequate income	Information on social and supplementary welfare
Counselling	Counselling
Support	Support and follow-up

Settlement Stage

The ultimate goal is to establish a permanent home which is secure and adequate, and is located in a community where there is ongoing support and the opportunity for friendship and participation in a new community. The task of moving home for any family or person is difficult and stressful. It is particularly so for those who are poor and have inadequate income, information and social contact.

They need practical help with establishing and maintaining a home, that is, with the furnishing of their home, budgeting, cooking and fuel bill management. If this help is not available, problems can arise in relation to rent arrears and outstanding debts, and feelings of dissatisfaction can develop which, in turn, can lead quickly to instability and insecurity once again. Some families and persons may need regular ongoing support from the personal social services such as individual counselling, or family therapy; others may need practical forms of help such as provision of home-making and home help services, day care services, meals-on-wheels and so forth.

166

Everyone needs information regarding their new neighbourhood and location of community resources. They also need a personal introduction to the area and someone to make them feel welcome. The absence of this process makes it very difficult for vulnerable families and individuals to settle in their new neighbourhood.

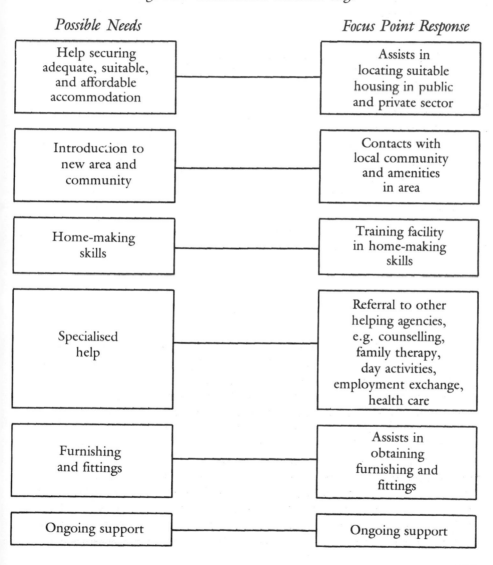

Fig. 18.5 Homelessness: Settlement Stage

Possible Needs	*Focus Point Response*
Help securing adequate, suitable, and affordable accommodation	Assists in locating suitable housing in public and private sector
Introduction to new area and community	Contacts with local community and amenities in area
Home-making skills	Training facility in home-making skills
Specialised help	Referral to other helping agencies, e.g. counselling, family therapy, day activities, employment exchange, health care
Furnishing and fittings	Assists in obtaining furnishing and fittings
Ongoing support	Ongoing support

167

Focus Point's Experience

Between September 1985 and September 1986, Focus Point helped some 110 people (seventy three women, thirty seven men) find accommodation in the private rented and public housing sectors. From this experience, Focus Point is aware of some of the significant factors which make the creation of a new home stable or unstable. Of the 110 people the agency helped to settle some sixty seven are still in that accommodation. In the cases where people were effectively settled, there were the following features:

– they had the opportunity to plan and prepare for their new home;

– they received regular ongoing support from social workers and home-makers;

– they were in a neighbourhood where they had friends and social contacts, or were well received by the neighbours;

– their tenancy was secure;

– the cost of their weekly rent was not excessive of their means.

Fig. 18.6

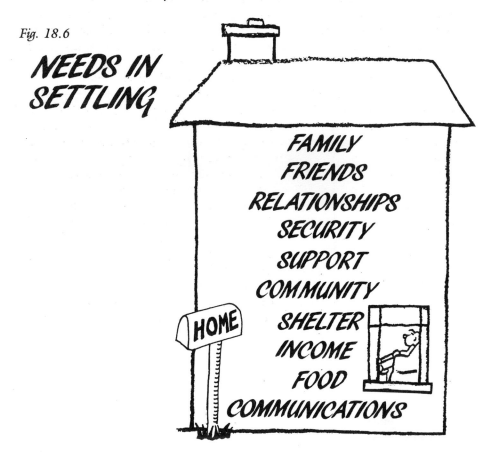

NEEDS IN SETTLING

FAMILY
FRIENDS
RELATIONSHIPS
SECURITY
SUPPORT
COMMUNITY
SHELTER
INCOME
FOOD
COMMUNICATIONS

HOME

Tom's Story

Tom is one person whom Focus Point helped to settle back in the community. His story illustrates the various stages of homelessness and what factors helped him settle in a community. Tom is sixty years old and came to Focus Point looking for accommodation. He had been staying in a bed and breakfast. He tells his own story:

I used to have a Corporation flat in the city centre but every few weeks I'd come home after walking around town only to find the place vandalised completely. I didn't mind too much the first time but after it happened again and again, I really got so afraid that one day I just decided to go. I took what little savings I had and went to a B&B. I had enough money for about three weeks there – after that there was nothing.

I heard about Focus Point from a social worker and went up there one day. I was very nervous because I didn't know the people, but they were very friendly and one of the workers came down with me to the Corporation and explained what had happened. I made an application there and then, I used to come down to Focus Point nearly every day and they'd send me up to the Corporation even on the days I didn't want to go.

I was fed up to tell you the truth! About two weeks after I heard I was to get a flat. I was delighted but I didn't know anyone in the area where the flat was so that worried me a bit. One of the Focus Point people took me around to some of the local people. The warden of the flats then gave me information on special services there for elderly people. So before I moved I nearly felt like it was my home already. The flat didn't have any furniture at all so it was really bare and awful. I didn't even have a plate to my name as I left all that in the last place. The same Focus Point person advised me to go to my Community Welfare Officer for furniture. I got some things: two plates, one knife, one spoon, one table, and a small cooker. I think he was hoping I wouldn't have any visitors. The next day they asked me to go back to the Welfare Officer because I was entitled to more things. I really got tired of all the comings and goings! I didn't get any more. I had to go to the Vincent de Paul. So I'm all set up now and am really happy.

I used to get sick very often, I think it was because I was so afraid. The people from Focus Point now call each week and I'm always glad to see them.

Consideration for the
Development of a Comprehensive Settlement Statutory Agency
in Dublin.

The current process of acquiring a tenancy in the public or private sector in Dublin is random, which gives little opportunity for planning an approach to combat homelessness.

Fig. 18.7 Where Were they Housed?

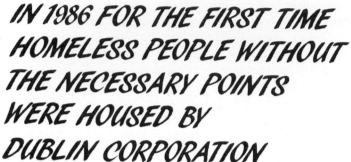

IN 1986 FOR THE FIRST TIME HOMELESS PEOPLE WITHOUT THE NECESSARY POINTS WERE HOUSED BY DUBLIN CORPORATION

HOMELESS INDIVIDUALS ▲ 780

HOMELESS SINGLE PARENT FAMILIES ● 988

HOMELESS TWO PARENT FAMILIES ■ 820

WHERE WERE THEY HOUSED?

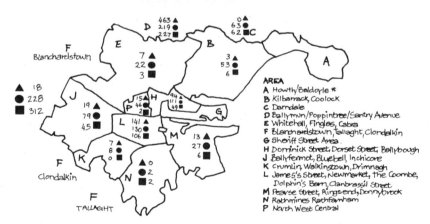

AREA
A Howth/Baldoyle *
B Kilbarrack, Coolock
C Darndale
D Ballymun/Poppintree/Santry Avenue
E Whitehall, Finglas, Cabra
F Blanchardstown, Tallaght, Clondalkin
G Sheriff Street Area
H Dominick Street, Dorset Street, Ballybough
J Ballyfermot, Bluebell, Inchicore
K Crumlin, Walkinstown, Drimnagh
L James's Street, Newmarket, the Coombe, Dolphin's Barn, Clanbrassil Street.
M Pearse Street, Ringsend, Donnybrook
N Rathmines Rathfarnham
P North West Central

* DUBLIN COUNTY COUNCIL HOUSING AREA.

170

(a) Local Authority Housing — Dublin Corporation

5. The Corporation allocation of tenancies is often random, being dependent on the immediate availability of a tenancy and the need of the Corporation to place new tenants there in order to prevent vandalism or squatting.

6. Allocation of tenancies can be very hurried, leaving little time to prepare and plan for this with a family or individual.

7. The allocation of tenancies to single persons, single parent families and homeless families are in hard to let areas and therefore vulnerable groups are becoming concentrated in these areas. This reinforces the people's sense of powerlessness, stigma and exclusion.

8. Many of those who are homeless have little or no household furnishings or furniture. The assistance received under the exceptional needs payments in the Supplementary Welfare Allowance Scheme in many cases is pitifully inadequate.

   In practice Focus Point has found that people may only obtain a small number of household items. As they have not the finance to furnish a home, they are made dependent on charities for secondhand furniture.

In 1986, for the first time, Dublin Corporation housed as many as 780 single homeless people, 988 single parent families and 820 homeless two parent families. These people tended to be housed together in low demand areas (as can be seen in Fig. 18.7). It should be noted that the term homeless is used by Dublin Corporation in relation to people who do not have the necessary points to be housed.

(b) The Private Rented Sector

In the private rented sector, there are a number of problems in acquiring a tenancy.

1. Good quality furnished accommodation is not available to people who are homeless and on low income. In consequence, therefore, people who have been homeless acquire tenancies at the lower end of the sector, where there is poor quality accommodation, over-crowded and shared facilities.

2. Low income and homeless groups at the lower end of the sector experience insecurity of tenure. Focus Point research established that tenants in this sector tend not to have leases or rent books (Focus Point, 1986).

3. The process of acquiring financial assistance from the Community Welfare Officer for a rent deposit and rent allowance is slow and inadequate, unreliable and at the discretion of the Community Welfare Officer. For example, a person moving from a hostel to a flat will have minimal income on which to maintain himself/herself for a number of weeks.

4. The areas of the city where low quality private rented accommodation is located

171

have few community resources and activities, and little opportunity for involvement locally.

What is needed

First, it must be acknowledged that the vast majority of people who find themselves out-of-home are ordinary people.

Second, some of these individuals and families can very quickly get caught in a cycle of homelessness, powerlessness and poverty unless they are offered *special services* which will enable them to move back into the mainstream of society rather than services which reinforce their isolation and exclusion.

Third, a Housing Advice, Information and Settlement Centre for individuals and families (such as the one being established by Focus Point) should be properly funded as a joint project of the Dublin Corporation Housing Department, Focus Point and the Eastern Health Board. The centre would be specifically geared to provide help to individuals and families who have special needs. Prior to the establishment of such a centre, research should be carried out on the settlement, support and voluntary groups in the city.*

The Housing Advice, Information and Settlement Centre would provide the following:
— Assessment of the needs of people out-of-home.
— Advice and information to those who are homeless on the housing options available to them.
— Counselling and support to individuals and families.
— Liaison and referral between the exisiting hostels in the city.
— Assistance with acquiring new accommodation.
— Assistance with moving into and establishing new homes and ongoing support where required.
— Liaison with organisations and agencies offering opportunities for work and leisure in the area of residency.
— Liaison and communicating with the neighbourhood and communities where people are being housed.
— The development of a positive community response to people who have been out-of-home and are newly settled in the area.

Fourth, the enactment of the Housing (Miscellaneous Provisions) Bill, 1985.

Fifth, a commitment is needed to a White Paper on Housing Policy in Ireland which would establish more accurately the nature and extent of need and the ways

*Since writing this paper a six month research project is being undertaken by Focus Point to examine the settlement, support and strategies of statutory and voluntary agencies and to make recommendations with regard to the future comprehensive settlement of socially vulnerable groups in Dublin. This project is being funded by the Combat Poverty Agency, is directed by Focus Point and advised by a Committee representing relevant statutory and voluntary agencies.

these needs may be met. This would include a strategy for the settlement of socially vulnerable individuals and families. It would also aim to contribute to a more integrated and cohesive society.

Such a Paper would include a commitment to social housing, assisted independent living units, the revitalisation of the private rented sector giving security of tenure to occupants, and a more equitable and realistic system of rent subsidies.

Finally, we need a commitment from the Government to carry out comprehensive research to discover the nature and extent of homelessness in Ireland over a one year period with continued monitoring. Policies are all too often based on misperception, prejudice and inadequate information.

Ultimately, however, unless we recognise each person's basic right to housing which is adequate, secure and affordable, and a right to community which facilities participation rather than isolation, the question of settling people who are out-of-home cannot be addressed realistically.

Appendix 18.1.
The Glasgow Experience

In spite of the differences between housing in Glasgow and housing in Dublin, much can be learned from the Glasgow experience of resettling homeless persons (Glasgow Council for Single Homeless, 1985). Glasgow, through combined housing and social intervention, has been able to respond effectively to individuals and families who are homeless. Glasgow is similar in size of population to Dublin, with a population of one million people. There is, however, a significant difference with regard to housing. Glasgow District Council has 170,000 housing units; Dublin Corporation has approximately 36,000 units. The private rented sector in Glasgow is small, expensive and inaccessible to homeless people. In Dublin, the private rented sector is larger and single homeless people are largely dependent upon it. In Glasgow under the 1977 Homeless Persons Act, it is the statutory obligation of the local authority to provide housing for homeless families and individuals.

In 1978, there were approximately 3,000 people living in hostels in Glasgow city. The District Council decided that hostel dwellers should be a priority group for housing under the 1977 Homeless Persons Act. The Housing Department agreed to embark on a policy of rehousing men and women from hostels and all applications from hostels would be directed through a Homeless Persons Unit which was established within the Housing Department. The Housing Persons Unit is a special unit within the Housing Department established specifically to help rehouse hostel dwellers. This unit is a joint project of the Social Work and the Housing Departments.

The Single Homeless Project provided practical support, assistance and encouragement to men and women being rehoused. This involved pre-housing training and preparation together with continued support, especially during the transition period.

The main instrument of this support was and is the provision of a home-maker service. The service is introduced to the applicant some 6-8 weeks before an offer of housing. This period allows the home-maker to assist the person in preparing to live independently such as budgeting, cooking, shopping, fuel bill management and making social contacts. The home-makers give intensive support to the person when he/she actually moves into the new homes and will then support him/her for approximately a further 3-6 months. Prior to support being terminated, the social worker and home-maker will visit to complete a final assessment. *Since January 1980, approximately 2,000 men and women have been rehoused from hostels and lodging houses into mainstream tenancies.*

One half of those rehoused have received some form of support from the Single Homeless Project, and one third have received the formal support of a home-maker. Research has established that the vast majority (upwards of 70%) of people have remained in their new homes, with 90% reporting that they were managing well. Only 2% of those originally rehoused had been identified as having returned to the hostels and being homeless.

What is clear from this experiment is that the Single Homeless Project has interpreted the 1977 Homeless Persons Act liberally; that it has given priority for housing to socially deprived and vulnerable groups, such as hostel dwellers and young persons aged 16-17 years; and by giving social work assistance many people were enabled to establish a home in the community. This combination of policies has proved to be very successful in setting resettlement people in the community.

References

Focus Point, 'A Study on Tenants in the Low Cost Private Rented Sector in Dublin', Unpublished, Focus Point, 1986, Dublin.
Glasgow Council for Single Homeless, *Rehousing Hostel Residents — the Experience in Glasgow*, 1985, Glasgow.

Housing policy for the future

This section puts into context the previous chapters by considering the problem of homelessness within the terms of policy issues. For a number of reasons, the problem of homelessness is inseparable from the outcome of housing policy as a whole. John Blackwell views homelessness in its widest sense which means it is not just lack of shelter but it comprises any type of marginalisation which occurs as a result of the operation of the housing system. He points out that a large volume of Exchequer funds is used for housing, both explicitly and, via tax consessions, implicitly, but only a negligible portion of it is earmarked for homelessness.

It is clear from Frank Convery's chapter, from the recommendations made by the authors and the seminar participants, that any resolution of the homelessness problem requires an approach to many aspects of housing policy: not just house building but allocation, administration, follow-up in the forms of settlement strategy, liaison between the housing authorities and other concerned agencies.

CHAPTER 19

Is there a need for change in housing policy?

John Blackwell

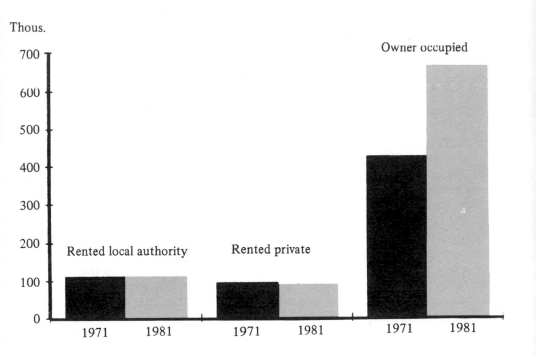

Thous.

Housing stock by tenure.

Introduction

The key question which is addressed in this chapter is whether Irish housing policy, as it has evolved since the last White Paper of 1969, is adequate to resolve the problems of homelessness in their widest sense. The chapter begins by examining the aims of housing policy. What is meant by homelessness and has its nature changed over time? The change in Irish housing conditions over the past fifteen years is then considered. How have housing policies coped with the persistent problem of homelessness? The extent to which marginal groups have lost out is examined. The underlying reasons for homelessness are then taken up. Finally, the housing policy issues which arise are outlined.

Aims of Housing Policy

The basic objective of Irish housing policy was stated in the 1969 White Paper to be "to ensure that, as far as the resources of the economy permit, every family can obtain for their occupation a house of good standard at a price or rent they can afford" (Ireland, 1969). This policy objective has remained (e.g., Department of Environment, 1983), replacing family by household, adding that the house be located in an acceptable environment, and significantly with the addition of a secondary aim. This is the encouragement of owner occupation. Significantly, the issue of income distribution has never been mentioned. This is despite the fact that housing policy has considerable impact on equity whether this is assessed in terms of equal treatment of equals (e.g. do households of similar income and household type receive broadly equal benefits in different housing sectors?) or in terms of income redistribution (e.g. do lower income households receive relatively higher benefits than others?). Much of the focus in official responses has been on the subsidy to those in the local authority letting tenure, and the need for adjustment here tends to be cited in terms of the pressures on Exchequer finances; rarely is there an advertance to the magnitude of the subsidy flows to owner occupiers.

Furthermore, objectives which are couched in such general terms cannot avoid begging some of the key questions. What is meant by a house of good standard? And what about the conflicts which can arise between the achievement of the different objectives, given the constraints which exist (in terms of resources which are available and the public finances)?

A particular instance of this has been the elevation of owner-occupation to such an important aim of housing policy. This has occurred in such an uncritical fashion that the relation between that drive – which has pushed owner-occupation to a current level of 75%, some twenty percentage points above the EEC average – and the achievement of shelter aims has never been queried at official level.

Yet another problem with such objectives is that they do not handle the trade-offs which exist between the different dimensions of housing. A house brings with it a bundle of services of different qualities: in terms of the physical structure of the dwelling, space, the security of tenure, quality of the neighbourhood, access to work and to services, potential for mobility. How does one compare a structurally

178

solid dwelling in a deteriorating neighbourhood with a structurally unfit dwelling in a stable neighbourhood?

This all implies that housing policy has to take in a wider set of issues than those which are narrowly related to housing quality or even housing costs. These include accessibility and the overall quality of the neighbourhood.

The difficulty in deciding on what are the aims of intervention in housing – to correct for inefficiency, redistribute income, affect Exchequer flows, boost owner-occupation, aid the construction industry? – has been thrown into sharp relief by the policies towards local authority lettings since the early 1970s.

The high take-up of the generous sales schemes is evidenced by the fact that the stock of local authority dwellings increased slightly from 112,700 in April 1971 to around 119,000 in 1986, despite aggregate completions of 95,300 in the period 1971-1985 inclusive. Hence, the contrast between the proportion of local authority dwellings in total completions – 23% on average over 1980-1986 inclusive, for instance – and their proportion in the total stock of some 12%. The policy has led in particular to considerable numbers of sales in the older local authority areas. In the Dublin sub-region, this has had the result that the availability of lettings has been increasingly concentrated on the outskirts of the urban area and on the poorer part of the dwelling stock. While the social mix may have been improved, there has been a reduced availability of dwellings for letting in particular areas. Hence, the ability of local authorities to meet their letting obligations may have been hampered. The opportunities for moves within local authority housing have been more spatially concentrated than was previously the case.

Another example concerns the £5,000 grant for local authority tenants who surrendered their dwellings to the local authority, abolished in the Budget of March 1987. While this may have been designed principally to reduce the waiting lists, it had adverse social consequences which are outlined below.

What is Meant by 'Homelessness'?

Over time, there has been an increasing recognition of the problem of homelessness, though up to recently there was little to be observed in official responses to housing problems. Ten or fifteen years ago, homelessness did not appear as a problem. It was not even the responsibility of the housing authorities, falling instead to the Health Boards, although in practice the responsibility was not clearly assigned to either Health Boards or Housing Authorities.

There was some recognition of cases which would now be counted in comprehensive definitions of homelessness. Local authorities have had responsibility for housing those "otherwise (i.e. other than unfitness, overcrowding, involuntary sharing) in need of housing on compassionate, medical or other similar grounds". This relates to Section 44 of the Housing Act 1966* which states that contributions may be made by the Minister to certain annual loan

*As amended in the Housing (Miscellaneous Provisions) Act, 1979.

charges of housing authorities, *inter alia,* "for the accommodation of persons who are in need of housing on medical, compassionate or other similar grounds if the circumstances of the persons would not permit them to be otherwise housed". An estimate for early 1980s was of a stock of some 4,000 households in this category, with of course a certain number of households entering the category each year.

If a distinction is made between home, house and household, this can serve as a useful prelude to an outline of the changing perceptions of homelessness over time. A house has a physical and spatial dimension. A household is a unit of organisation which is distinct to the home. A home is where that unit is usually constituted and is physically located. The home is that locale where the individual, the household and society interact. At one stage, homelessness was seen as the same as 'houselessness'. This view of homelessness has gradually given way to one which views homelessness as occurring wherever people live in conditions which exclude them from the type of housing conditions enjoyed by the majority of households.

Just as poverty has come to be seen as reflecting relative disparities in levels of living, as much as absolute deficiencies in living standards, so also homelessness reflects the inequalities in housing provision.

The Outcome since 1969 — a Success Story?

For Irish households as a whole, their housing conditions on average have improved notably over the past fifteen years. The evidence for this can be summed up as follows.

While age is not always a good indicator of unfitness, there is a relation between the age of dwelling and fitness. Given the rate of home completions in the past fifteen years, about 42% of the housing stock must now be under fifteen years of age. The increase over time in rates of dwelling completion per 1000 population can be seen as follows:

Table 19.1
Dwelling Completions per 1,000 Population, 1970, 1975, 1980-1986

Year	Completions
1970	4.7
1975	8.5
1980	8.2
1981	8.4
1982	7.7
1983	7.5
1984	7.1
1985	6.8
1986	6.4

The proportion of dwellings which lack basic amenities has declined, judging by the presence of water supply and sanitary facilities. The average size of dwellings has increased. While it is true that the decline in real incomes which has occurred since 1979 has taken its toll, the average size of dwellings being completed – which increased by 16% between 1970 and 1979 and then fell in each subsequent year but one – is still higher (by 9%) than it was in 1980. The 1980 Survey of the Housing Stock found that 8.3% of housing units in the State were unfit compared with 11.7% in 1973.

The quality of dwellings in the local authority tenure has improved. Physical standards and design standards (at least in certain urban areas) have improved; the average number of rooms per dwelling and their average size have increased.

The incidence of overcrowding has declined. Using a very conservative measure of two or more persons per room, the number of overcrowded households was 54,400 in 1971 and had fallen to 26,000 by 1981. As a proportion of all households, the proportion overcrowded fell from 7.5% to 2.9% in this period. Some of these households contain three or more persons per room – their number was 3,200 in 1981 compared with 9,100 in 1971, again a substantial decrease. It has been argued that overcrowding can be defined as *more than* 1.5 persons per room (Blackwell, 1983).

If this criterion were adopted, then the number of overcrowded households in 1981 would be 52,400 rather than 26,000. The 1980 Housing Survey showed 21.8% of housing units in contravention of Section 63 of the Housing Act, 1966, most of them due to air-space violations. Of the stock, 2.5% of units contained households where bedroom privacy criteria are violated and about 2% to 3% of units contained households where not only are privacy standards not met, but there are lower standards of facilities together with a higher incidence of unfitness.

The proportion of dwellings with more than one family, which is an indicator of housing stress as it often shows involuntary doubling up, has declined. The number of multi-family households declined from 25,200 in 1971 to 20,200 in 1981 and can be assumed to have declined further since then. It is not known how much of the above sharing is involuntary, nor is it known how many of these households comprise married couples living with their in-laws, although it is likely that many of them are in this category. The Housing Survey 1980 shows that 9,590 households contained involuntary sharing. In the case of such multi-family households, the 'concealed households' which occur are either married couples with parents-in-law, or lone-parent families living with others who desire independent accommodation.

Single persons who wish to set up separate accommodation have formerly not been regarded as a part of housing requirements. This reflects the letting priorities of local authorities, taken up below. Again, this raises the question of what the stated aims of housing policy mean by "every household (obtaining) . . . a house of good standard . . .". Current practice counts a family unit which shares a dwelling involuntarily as part of housing 'need' but does not count a single person who shares a dwelling involuntarily. Each of these cases involves a 'concealed' or potential household which will become an actual household only if backed up by effective demand, or if allocated a local authority dwelling.

The evident desire of people for independence, not just among family type households, but among single persons who formerly might have lived at home, and among elderly people who formerly might have shared a dwelling with in-laws, continues to be felt. This is despite the fall in real incomes which has occurred since 1979. Between 1979 and 1986, disposable personal incomes per head – that is, after-tax household incomes from all sources – in real terms fell by 9%. In the same period, after tax earnings of those at work, on average industrial earnings, fell by 12% in real terms in the case of single people. A degree of social momentum has been achieved with regard to 'household fission', whereby young and older members of the extended family split off and form independent households.

A feature of the 1971-81 period was the marked rise in rates of household formation among single persons – partly reflecting economic forces and partly reflecting changes in social mores. It is notable that rates of household formation have, it seems, continued to increase beyond 1979, despite the adverse trends in income. This has been one of the elements beyond the marked rise in the number of one-person households which has continued beyond 1981. Between 1971 and 1981, one person households recorded the biggest percentage increase of any household type, one of 47.2%, by contrast with 23.4% for all households. Between 1981 and 1986, one-person households increased in number by 16.1%, by contrast with an increase of 7.2% for all households. This is likely to have reflected both the rise in marginal tax rates among single persons and a degree of social momentum which has been reflected in household fission.

In the 1970s, owner occupiers who were in their early years of a mortgage tended to have higher repayments relative to income – a product of high interest rates. However, with the high inflation rates of that period, the real burden of repayments declined marginally over time. One disquieting trend of the 1980s is that the rise in real interest rates, decline in inflation rates and the recession have combined to alter this feature markedly now. The repayments relative to income show a much slower decline over time. While the Housing Finance Agency has made it easier for lower income households to fund a mortgage, there remains a concern that buyers who were just able to fund a loan may face difficulties in being able to fund repayments.

Finally, it should be noted that such successes as occurred were stimulated through a significant expenditure of Exchequer funds. A rough estimate of the total amount of housing subsidies in 1986 is £460 million. This includes the so-called tax expenditures or losses in tax revenue due to special tax provisions which are designed to favour the consumption of housing. Suppose, as an imaginary experiment, that these subsidies were converted into a per household cash grant per annum, averaged, say, over all households except those who own outright. The average cash grant per household, covering rich and poor alike, would be £1,200 per annum at 1986 prices.

Some People Untouched by Improvements

Despite the improvement in housing conditions which many Irish households experienced, there has been an increasing disparity between the quality of housing services obtained by most households, and that obtained by those at the bottom end of the housing market. In other words, there has been an increasing duality in Irish housing conditions. This can be seen from the fact that certain people have benefitted little, or not at all, from the general improvement in housing conditions over the past decade or so.

This is indicated by the stagnation, or even disimprovement in housing conditions which has occurred among those with the poorest quality dwelling or with none at all. This is evidenced by the following:

– the persistence of unfitness and of overcrowding;

– the evident decay in part of the private letting sector;

– the number of persons living in temporary housing units, i.e. essentially mobile homes, in recent years: 29,100 (in 11,400 households) in 1986;

– the thousands of homeless people, including those squatting in local authority dwellings;

– the impact of the lack of security of tenure and of relatively high housing costs in relation to income in much of the private letting sector;

– the lack of basic facilities among certain elderly persons who live alone (Power, 1980) and the housing problems of the elderly poor.

Some of the disparities in housing conditions are related to difficulties in obtaining access to housing. Those families which are unable to finance housing from their own resources are dependent on the local authority sector for accommodation. There have been distinct differences between areas in the ease with which such accommodation can be obtained, especially for young families. At least up to recently, until the take-up of the £5,000 'surrender' grant reduced considerably the waiting list for local authority lettings, families could have been driven to show 'need' for local authority housing by living in overcrowded or multi-family conditions; hence, some of the overcrowding and involuntary sharing was a likely reflection of the letting criteria of local authorities. Others have not qualified for local authority lettings, even though they live in poor housing, because they are not eligible, as in the case of many single people aged under sixty. Currently, local authority dwellings are not allocated to non-family units, unless they are elderly single persons or are disabled persons or suffer from particular forms of ill-health.

Some of the lower income households in privately rented accommodation have consisted of families queuing for a local authority dwelling. Others have consisted of those who, although not eligible for local authority loans, may never be able to raise the deposit for, and repay a loan from, a building society. The conditions of those in the private letting sector, typified by the conditions in the Dublin sub-region, have given rise to considerable concern and have been well documented by Threshold (e.g., O'Brien and Dillon, 1982). The polarisation in this tenure between high income households with high quality accommodation at one end and low income households spending a relatively high proportion of their income on housing at the other end, makes this tenure a microcosm of Irish housing conditions. However, it is not just that the households in this tenure spend more on housing as a proportion of income than that of any other tenure group (some 15% of disposable income for the lower income household in this tenure, by contrast with 7% for all households). In addition, those at the bottom end of the private letting tenure obtain a relatively poor quality of housing services and have a considerable degree of insecurity. This reflects in part the economic weakness of the tenants. It also reflects the impacts of housing and urban policies. Private letting tenants have been squeezed between their own economic weakness and a shrinking supply of adequate accommodation.

In turn, that shrinking supply has reflected the following:
1. the loss of, first, higher-income and in recent years, middle-income demand to owner-occupation;
2. the loss of low to moderate income family demand to the public sector;
3. to some extent, losses of public sector housing due to slum clearance.

On the last point, one of the greatest difficulties which urban policy faces in areas such as Dublin is that in the city core, the only gross additions to housing stock occur through public sector housing.

In urban areas such as Dublin, some residential accommodation has either fallen into decay, become vacant or been converted to more lucrative use. The latter has involved either high density apartments for the upper end of the market or else office use. In the inner suburbs of Dublin, where once there were dwellings available to residents of modest incomes within easy access of their place of work, commercial developments and provision of dwellings for those on higher incomes have limited the availability of housing. Thus, the continuation of weakness in effective demand, insecurity of tenure, losses to the stock on the supply side, and uncertainty about the future of this tenure – in part because of a lack of commitment on the part of policy makers – have all combined to make this tenure even more of a marginal one than it was ten or fifteen years ago. In 1971, of a total of 127,000 housing units in Dublin County Borough, 22,509 or 17.7% were rented in the private sector. In 1981, of a total of 137,500 units in the Borough, 20,000 or 14.5% were rented in the private sector.

Who are the Homeless?

The perceptions of the homeless have often been as a group of vagrants, predominantly male, aged over forty. Such perceptions have existed both in Ireland

184

and in other countries ('skid row'). However, such perceptions are often misplaced. Whether defined in the narrow sense of 'houselessness' or in the more broad sense, the homeless are not a homogeneous group. They include families and single persons, increasingly women and increasingly persons aged under forty. They include the single homeless, who live in hostels and night shelters and who sleep rough in places such as public parks. Many of the homeless do not differ from the 'ordinary' families who are on local authority waiting lists – except in the degree of desperation of their housing conditions.

The homeless are at the bottom end of the housing market, not just in terms of quality of housing but in terms of the choices open to them. For instance, family units may be forced to split up, with some forming multi-family households. Some of this sharing accounts for the 'hidden' homeless. It may be necessary for families to split up in order to secure some type of accommodation. An important aspect of housing quality is the availability of choice – in terms of type of dwelling, location, degree of discretion with regard to management and improvement of the dwelling in the case of tenants, opportunities for mobility.

A graphic instance of the importance of this dimension can be observed from the take-up of the £5,000 grant in the local authority tenure. The take-up of this grant in the Dublin sub-region area was concentrated in Tallaght, Darndale, Clondalkin and Blanchardstown (Threshold, 1987). This suggests that dissatisfaction with housing locations within the local authority tenure is concentrated in certain areas.

Little firm data are available on the number of homeless. Current estimates cover only those in the most deprived group who are 'houseless' and does not include, for instance, those who may be threatened with eviction in the private letting sector or those families who share a dwelling with another family, or those living in hostels, many of whom should be considered homeless; nor does it include the 15,000-20,000 Travellers. In any counting of the homeless, it is important to distinguish between stocks and flows. Estimates such as those cited above relate to a stock at a point in time. However, the number of people who are touched by homelessness at some time would be greater than this, as people enter and leave this state. While there is a margin of error about the stock estimates, the numbers of homeless have been increasing over time.

The public perceptions of the homeless matter. If the homeless are seen as vagrants who are outside society, housing policy may be regarded as having nothing to do with them. This has in fact been the position in Ireland. Housing policy concerned itself hardly at all with the problem of homelessness, and the housing authorities were not seen as having a role to play in dealing with this problem.

Reasons for Homelessness
While it is worthwhile to establish the characteristics of the homeless, it is necessary to go beyond this – to inquire what are the underlying reasons for homelessness. This is crucially important: what are the structural features of the

housing market which result in homelessness? Unless this question is attacked, the stereotype of the homeless as vagrants and winos can lead to the conclusion that these people are homeless due to 'their own' fault — due to their fecklessness and their having opted out of society.

The reasons for homelessness can be divided into economic reasons and social reasons, as follows:

Economic
1. The immediate causes cover cases such as eviction, or where householders are unable to pay rent increases, or where rent arrears have built up.
2. More fundamental causes would include unemployment, inability to exist on social welfare benefits, and (on the supply side of housing) the reduction which has occurred in the supply of dwellings in the private letting tenure.

Social
1. Cases where persons wish to escape from actual or potential conflicts in households: here there can be a link between domestic turmoil and inadequate housing conditions such as overcrowding or enforced sharing.
2. Inability or unwillingness of parents, relatives and friends to accommodate people.
3. Cases where young people leave home in order to achieve independence: some of these cases may result in short-term spells of homelessness.
4. Cases where people are released from institutions and where there is no home through which they can rejoin society.
5. Cases of marital breakdown and cases of battered wives.

Why have the Numbers of Homeless Increased?
There are a number of reasons why the numbers of homeless persons have increased over time.
— There has been a change over time in the pattern of migration. In the 1950s and 1960s, Irish homelessness was in evidence in Britain. It is noteworthy that many of the homeless whom the Milner Holland Committee on Housing in Greater London spoke to twenty one years ago came from Ireland and other countries other than Britain, (Committee on Housing in Greater London, 1965). By the mid 1970s this pattern of migration had changed to one of net in-migration. The current turn around in migration is of a different character from that of the 1950s, with a much higher skill content.
— Labour market conditions have changed and the casual work on which some of the homeless depended is no longer to be had in urban areas.
— There has been increasing incidence of marital breakdown and an increasing number of lone parent families, which are one of the most vulnerable groups with regard to housing conditions. The Threshold data show that homelessness was more prevalent among lone parents, the separated and the widowed, than

186

among any other marital status group (O'Brien and Dillon, 1982). From the Census of Population, incidentally, it is almost impossible to trace the increased incidence of lone parent families. (This is partly because of the *de facto* nature of the Census, which does not count people on the basis of their usual residence but rather on their actual residence 'on the night', partly because lone parents who live with their parent(s) will tend to be hidden in the Census tables, and partly because the family unit tabulations in the Census date only from 1979.)

— Given that homelessness is closely connected with poverty and unemployment, the rise in rates of unemployment and the concentration of unemployment in certain areas have led to homelessness.

Links between Homelessness and Housing Policy

There are a number of key links between homelessness and housing policy in general.

First, if the wider definition of homelessness is used, this means that many aspects of housing policy other than simply building targets have a bearing on homelessness: such as allocation policy, housing administration and the effectiveness with which the housing authorities work with other agencies such as social service departments and agencies. The importance of liaison between the housing authorities and social service bodies arises, because some homelessness reflects not so much a physical shortage of housing as a lack of support which in instances people get from families or from the wider community.

Second, there are particularly acute problems in urban areas and in the inner city areas, some of which have to do with lack of appropriate housing provision, and some which reflect wider problems of urban decay and declines of certain industries and trades which were once a feature of the urban areas.

Third, there is a need to distinguish those cases where homeless persons never had a secure dwelling of their own from cases where they lost occupation of dwelling. The former cases can reflect either physical shortage of housing *or* difficulties of access to suitable housing. Of course, there are likely to be interactions here between housing shortages and a consequent tendency for housing authorities to impose restrictive conditions for entry into local authority housing.

Fourth, changes in the private letting tenure (e.g. reduction in supply) and in owner occupation (e.g. loan default or inability to engage in repair) have an impact on the homeless.

Conclusions and Policy Issues

To some extent, Irish housing policy over the past fifteen years has been a story of success — a historically high rate of completions per capita has been achieved and the bulk of households have enjoyed a higher level of housing services. This has been achieved at some expense — in terms of Exchequer costs and losses of environmental quality (occurring through the ubiquitous ribbon development). More particularly in view of the theme here, it has been achieved at a time of widening inequalities in housing provision. Those at the bottom end of the housing ladder have suffered an absolute decline in housing standards, not just a relative disimprovement. Some lessons from this experience can surely be learned, as follows.

1. The development of housing policy in a piecemeal fashion which has occurred — the plugging of gaps, partly in response to vocal outcrys about housing conditions — means that groups such as the homeless, who lack political weight, remain at the bottom of the queue for housing. For 1986, housing subsidies in aggregate are estimated at some £460 million, a tiny fraction of which went towards the homeless. It also means that policy has evolved in a less than coherent fashion in a world where the efficacy of policy instruments in meeting the different objectives set for housing policy needs to be questioned. And there is a need to face up to trade-offs between the achievement of different objectives.

2. It might be thought that the provision of high quality dwellings at the upper end of the housing market will ultimately 'filter' down to improve those who live in the worst housing conditions. According to this story of 'filtering', the provision of new dwellings of good quality to high-income families leads to their vacating dwellings which become available to a lower income group, and so on along a chain of vacancies until the housing conditions of the poorest families are improved and slum dwellings are demolished. This filtering story simply does not work adequately in practice. It posits a smoothly working housing market, with good information among purchasers and sellers, which does not exist in reality. The chain of vacancies may break before the poorest families benefit much. The benefits do not percolate down to those with poorest housing conditions, least of all to the homeless.

3. The housing problems of the most deprived will not be overcome through new building alone. To this end, appropriate policies on housing allocation, administration and on the responsibilites which fall on the housing authorities are required. Many of the severe problems of rural unfitness which existed in the early 1960s have been overcome. Some, though not all, of overcrowding problems have been overcome, or have resolved themselves through the decline in family size which has occurred. There remain, however, acute problems of potential unfitness looming up in urban areas. Many of the most intractable housing problems which remain are a reflection of unemployment, poverty, and social exclusion, of which the stigmatisation of particular areas is but one dimension. Because of this, these problems require solutions other than simply building dwellings . To what extent can the existing pattern of housing aids be directed more at those people who are the most deprived, without incurring the take-up problems which are associated with means-tested benefits? The latter problems, whereby not all those who are eligible for benefit actually claim,

188

reflect stigma, lack of information and the expense which households may have to go to in order to claim benefit.

4. The ceaseless pushing up of owner-occupation as an end in itself has got to the point where it gets in the way of achieving other policy objectives. It can mean loss of flexibility in the use of the housing stock, as private letting dwellings, which can serve the young mobile population and students among others, are lost from the stock. And the policy can rebound – in a period of falling real incomes, households can get into difficulty in making repayments, repossessions and loan defaults occur and necessary repairs are deferred.

5. Arising from the foregoing point, the potential for a 'third arm' of housing, housing associations or housing co-operatives – working in conjunction with the public authorities – has been woefully underachieved in Ireland. Their potential role includes rehabilitation, the acquisition and conversion of older properties and greater tenant participation in management of housing.

6. The weakness of housing provision in inner city areas has in part been due to the difficulty of stimulating private investment in housing in such areas. With a sufficient level of public sector. investment, including in neighbourhood improvement, would the private sector follow?

7. The waiting list for local authority housing has declined markedly in recent years. In the period since 1977, the waiting list for Dublin Corporation peaked at 6,700 in 1981, was 6,700 in 1983 and fell to 4,500 by December 1985. The waiting list for Dublin County Council was 1,700 in December 1983 and fell to 800 by December 1985. This has reflected the take-up of the £5,000 grant together with the use of Housing Finance Agency loans. There has been a tendency to equate this with success in Irish housing policy. For a number of reasons, one should be slow to do this. First, local authority waiting lists are not synonymous with housing 'need'. Second, the concentration of households which are entirely dependent on social welfare payments in the local authority tenure together with the loss of those who could be expected to be among the most active and vocal tenants, has social implications.

The loss of tenants who might be expected to be community leaders leads to a less vibrant tenure, and makes it more likely than innovations such as devolution of management to tenants, would be handicapped at the outset. The result may be an acceleration of the process whereby the local authority letting tenure becomes a residual service, with a high degree of stigmatisation. The more tenants leave, the more this may result. It may be noted that, by 1985, 57% of tenants were dependent on social welfare payments.

Third, there is fragmentary evidence that vacancy rates have increased in recent years. Certainly the vacancy rates in the local authority tenure have increased markedly. This has reflected the number of tenants availing of the £5,000 grant for surrendering their dwellings to the local authority – and in particular the concentration of these cases in increasingly hard to let estates. High vacancy

189

rates, which are well beyond the 'frictional' rates of, say, 2% of the housing stock needed to make the housing market work smoothly, mean a notably inefficient use of housing stock.

Fourth, the take-up of the £5,000 grant suggests that tenants in certain estates in the Dublin sub-region have been dissatisfied with their housing location. There is currently a tendency to replace them by concentrations of marginal groups, such as lone-parent families and single persons who up to now would not have qualified for local authority housing. This trend may lead to a perpetuation of housing problems in estates which are becoming increasingly stigmatised. In particular, housing and other social problems are likely to multiply in such estates unless housing authorities work effectively with social service agencies. Thus, effective allocation policy, settlement help after allocation and effective working with social service agencies, voluntary groups and co-operatives are all crucial to the effectiveness of the work of the housing authorities.

References

Blackwell, John, *Housing Requirements and Population Change, 1981-1991,* National Economic and Social Council, 1983, Dublin.
Committee on Housing in Greater London (Milner Holland), *Report, Cmnd. 2605,* HMSO, 1965, London.
Department of Environment, *The Human Settlement Situation and Related Trends and Policies: Ireland* 1983, Report to Economic Commission for Europe, 1983, Dublin.
Ireland, *Housing in the Seventies,* Stationery Office, 1969, Dublin.
O'Brien, L., and Dillon, B., *Private Rented: the Forgotten Sector,* Threshold, 1982, Dublin.
Power, B., *Old and Alone in Ireland,* Society of St. Vincent de Paul, 1980, Dublin.
Threshold, *Policy Consequences: A Study of the £5,000 Surrender Grant in the Dublin Housing Area,* Threshold, 1987, Dublin.

CHAPTER 20

A way forward

Frank Convery

Focus on Homelessness Seminar, organised by Focus Point,
Dublin, in January, 1987.
Left to right: Paddy Morrissey, Assistant City and County
Manager; Davy Byrne, Assistant City and County
Manager; Tom Corcoran, Department of the
Environment; Sr Stanislaus, Focus Point; Pat McDonnell,
Planning Section, Dublin Corporation.

Introduction

Here I offer some reactions to the foregoing chapters. This does not pretend to be a comprehensive set of conclusions but takes up some key elements.

A number of contributors – John Blackwell and others – mention the objectives, whether in the form of shelter or other aims, which have governed housing policy in recent years. An objective which might be compatible with what most contributors are saying would be this: to give a sense of community, self-worth and dignity to communities, families and individuals, without distinction as to origin or designation. If we set this objective, a new set of thought processes, initiatives and approaches would be triggered off. Arising from the contributions, there are several things that could be done in the existing policy framework, and there are a number of policy initiatives which might also be taken.

The Existing Policy Framework

First, we need to educate ourselves about our prejudices. In relation to many social issues, we have not gone through the heightening of consciousness whereby people view and appraise attitudes, views and preconceived notions.

As a result, I think, a lot of our reflexes are unconsciously very deficient and lead us in directions which are inimical to the development of the community. An important issue is how to educate ourselves in these matters.

Second, we could inform people more about the background to their choices and about their entitlements. Information, to a fundamental extent, is power. Those who know what the choices are and what their rights are, what the directions of change are, have greater confidence and ability to make good decisions. There are very encouraging initiatives in this area, such as those outlined by Pat McDonnell, but we could do enormously more on this front.

Third, we could do more to integrate existing policies. This is easy to say and is often recommended but it is not so easy to do. We all know that if you are trying to achieve something, the easiest way to get ahead is to push ahead without reference to what other people are doing. However, if the objective is the development of community, it means involving all facets of community and somehow keeping going forward while at the same time being open to influences which make the ideal of the community work. We have had several examples, from the case studies from Tallaght, Ballymun and so on, where it seems fairly obvious that the various elements in the development of community were not brought along simultaneously to a sufficient degree. I do not think it is an adequate excuse to say that the desired outcome will happen in thirty years or whenever.

Fourth, improvement is feasible in the area of design for living. This is in part a question of being sensitive to elements such as how you build a house, orientate it in terms of sunshine, cluster buildings, landscape areas. It is possible to achieve excellence in design if the highest calibre of design skills is used. We have seen what has been achieved in the inner city by contrast with what has not been achieved in several other locales, largely because the highest calibre of design skills were brought

192

to bear at the right time. It is less easy, of course, to apply design after the job has been done. High quality design from the beginning is critical, as is evident from the chapter by Philip Geoghegan. By comparison with other countries, our design quality is seriously deficient in terms of enhancing community. This deficiency seems to be part of our cultural endowment, but that is no reason to live with it forever.

Good design almost always saves money. If the right design skills are applied initially, the payback will exceed the additional cost several-fold.

One of the elements of design which is critical is the design of facilities to meet the needs of people in various circumstances. This may not involve spending more money but ensuring that it is money being spent on the right type of skills and facilities.

Fifth, an element which does cost money – and possibly this is one of the reasons why it has not happened – is service to the client. In several instances in the chapters there is reference to people being given housing or a place in a hostel and just being left to their own devices. Once again, the panoply of services that are required to succeed involve developing the community concept. This does require resources, but more importantly perhaps, it requires a fundamental attitude that this will happen and that it will be important.

Policy Initiatives

There are a number of policy initiatives where improvements are possible. First, there is the housing policy question. John Blackwell's expenditure estimate was very striking to me: the fact that there is an Exchequer transfer of £460 million a year going into the housing sector. This enormous sum can be allocated in several different ways. As we have heard several contributors point out, we have chosen to discriminate in the allocation of that money against the private rented sector in general and specifically against the existing building stock by comparison with the favouring of new building.

The kinds of incentives and procedures and investment policies that have been adopted, are directly related to the decline of the inner city community. The need for a White Paper in this area now is evident. As several contributors point out, choices have opened up because of the changes in the nature of the housing problem. We can start looking afresh at this entire area and I personally would favour a radical rethink, completely getting away from the large tracts of public housing on the one hand and private estates on the other. This polarisation is economically inefficient, environmentally deficient and socially unhealthy. Rather, we should move in the direction of community based housing, involving a public-private partnership.

Second, there is, as Bannon pointed out, an initiative which needs to be given some kind of statutory basis. This relates to participation, of somehow bringing the people who are most affected by change into the decision-making process. As in the case of integration of policies, the promotion of more local participation and local involvement should be encouraged for the benefit of all rather than small 'self interested' groups.

Third, there is the issue of local authority structure in the Dublin sub-region. The current reorganisation proposed involves breaking the Dubin area into four entities, which as far as I can see is meaningless from a community point of view, does not seem to capture any particular economies of scale and just creates another set of difficulties.

The idea of having a region-wide entity together with a cluster of much smaller community entities with which people can identify, has far more powerful and logical force. Such a structure, as advocated by Bannon, should facilitate participation. A useful example of what can be done comes from the Glasgow experience of resettling homeless people which was discussed in the chapter by Kennedy and O'Brien. This demonstrates the great effort which was put into involving all the different interests in order to deal with a particular problem, and to learn from each other as they develop. Thereby, the idealists become realists, the realists become mildly idealistic and proper decisions and mutual respect gradually develop.

Recommendations and Summary
of Discussion

Six main issues which caused concern to speakers and participants at the *Focus on Homelessness* Seminar in Dublin, 1987 were:
— The lack of adequate legislation in relation to housing and homelessness.
— The lack of adequate co-ordination and integration of administrative structures with regard to policy, planning, design and delivery of housing in the public, private rented and voluntary housing sector.
— The lack of appropriate community amenities, facilities and services, especially in low-demand areas and camping sites.
— The lack of adequate administrative structures which facilitate participation of residents and tenants in housing planning and policy.
— The inequity of housing subsidies and the lack of a coherent policy towards the private rented sector.
— The lack of research and public education regarding attitudes to and conditions of homeless and Travelling people.

There was a good deal of unanimity amongst participants that the following specific changes relating to these main issues should take place:

Legislation
— Work should begin immediately on a White Paper on housing policy in Ireland. This paper should estimate the nature and extent of housing needs and set out the way in which these needs should be met.
— The Housing (Miscellaneous Provisions) Bill, 1985 should be amended so that the rights of homeless people are protected.
— Effective regulations and standards regarding the conditions of renting in the private rented sector should be established to protect the rights of tenants and landlords and the community in general.
— The Children (Child and Protection) Bill, 1986 should be amended so that care, protection and housing may be provided for children and young people up to eighteen years of age.
— The needs of young people between sixteen and eighteen years of age who cannot remain in their own homes and are not in residential care should be met with a guaranteed form of income and maintenance under the Social Welfare Acts and with a wide range of different types of accommodation and housing offering different degrees of protection and independence. Assurance of after care services should be given to young people leaving residential care and who cannot return to their own homes. Health Boards should liaise with local

authority housing sections and relevant voluntary groups in making arrangments for this accommodation.

Planning and Administration

— Housing planning and policies in the future should take into account the rapid changes taking place in the social, demographic and family structures in Ireland.

— Appropriate housing administrative structures should be established to facilitate community participation at local level, giving all citizens a sense of dignity and worth in the community.

— If housing policy and practice is to be meaningful in the future, co-ordination should take place between policy makers, planners and those experiencing the effects of housing policy, planning and practice at local level.

— Rejuvenation and refurbishing of old housing stock especially in the city centre should be a part of any future plans for Dublin city.

— Housing subsidies should be reviewed and made more equitable in the public, owner occupied and private rented sector.

— Suitable design should be recognised as an important aspect of planning and should be an integral part of planning in the future.

Research

— Research should be carried out to determine the meaning, the nature and the extent of homelessness in Ireland.

— Research should be carried out to determine the precise housing needs and supports needed by socially vulnerable groups, i.e. people who spend a long time in institutions such as psychiatric hospitals, children's homes, those who have had traumatic experiences such as experiences of violence, exploitation, abandonment, rejection etc.

— Action research should be carried out on the accommodation needs of the Travelling people as they see them.

Services

— The quality of housing services, amenities and facilities should be improved notably in those areas which have gained little from the overall improvement in housing conditions which has occurred in recent years. This is especially needed in low-demand areas and in camping sites for Travelling people to ensure that the residents are given the quality of housing which is their lawful right and in keeping with their dignity as human beings.

— Planners should recognise that people need homes, and not merely houses, with all the security, peace and privacy which a home brings.

– Planners should also recognise that people need to live in communities and not merely in housing estates which lack some, and sometimes even all, forms of community participation and facilities.

Special Provisions
– A high proportion of present hostel residents could live in the community if appropriate accommodation was available for them.
– Some residents living in hostels need specialised treatment for psychiatric problems and different forms of addiction and need special types of care and accommodation rather than being left in hostels where there are not the resources available to meet their needs.
– For people who have been most of their lives in institutions and who are not likely to move out into the community, the existing accommodation provision could be renovated and upgraded so that they may provide accommodation that is as near as possible to a home-like atmosphere.
– Voluntary and non-profit housing should be recognised as a very important and integral part of housing in Ireland and should be planned for and funded adequately. The potential of this form of housing, especially for socially vulnerable groups such as elderly people, people leaving institutions and those groups mentioned above should be acknowledged.
– In the future, hostels should only be used as emergency and short term accommodation and should receive adequate funding to ensure they are of high standard and have appropriate staffing.
– Appropriate and proper housing information, advice and support centres should be promoted and funded in every city and town to help identify and integrate socially vulnerable people back into the community. These centres should take into account the varying needs of people, the degrees of independence that are appropriate for them and the support which they need in the community. The centres should be co-funded and managed by the relevant voluntary bodies, the housing authority and the health board.
– There should be close liaison between the health boards and housing authorities and relevant voluntary bodies regarding rent allowance, deposits, furnishings and home-making services.

Public Education
– Public education programmes funded and supported by the State should be carried out to inform and, where necessary, create understanding in relation to the homeless and Travelling people.
– Public education programmes funded and supported by the State should prepare people, particularly young people, for the time when they leave home.

197

Co-ordination

There should be co-ordination and a framework operating between the various Departments of Government at national, regional and local level and voluntary bodies to ensure that the best use is made of existing resources, that overlapping is reduced and in order to provide an integrated approach to the planning and the delivery of housing and allied services and amenities.

It is essential that future plans provide for mixed types of housing schemes with integrated groups and communities and discontinue the present system which is leading to marginalisation and disintegration rather than cohesive communities.

FOCUS ON HOMELESSNESS
Towards a White Paper on Housing Policy in Ireland.

For the International Year of Shelter for the Homeless.

SCHEDULE OF SEMINAR

Dates: Thursday 8th and Friday 9th January 1987. **Venue:** Riverside Centre, 8-11 Sir John Rogerson's Quay, Dublin 2.
Seminar Rapporteur: Professor Frank Convery, Department of Environmental Studies, University College Dublin.

Thursday 8th January:

TIME	TITLE	SPEAKER
7.00 p.m.	Welcome Opening Address	An Taoiseach, Dr. Garret FitzGerald
7.15 p.m.	Who are the Homeless?	Stanislaus Kennedy, *Focus Point*
7.30 p.m.	Housing Policy as related to Marginal Groups, particularly homeless groups in Dublin	John Blackwell, *Department of Environmental Studies, UCD.*
8.00 p.m.	Current Policy and Future Plans as Related to Marginal Groups	Paddy Morrissey, *Assistant City and County Manager*
8.15 p.m.	The Allocation of Houses by Dublin Corporation, particularly to homeless people	Aidan O'Sullivan, *Housing Allocation Section, Dublin Corporation.*
8.30 p.m.	Coffee/Tea	
8.45 p.m.	Open Discussion	
9.20 p.m.	Resumée	Professor Frank Convery, *Seminar Rapporteur.*
9.30 p.m.	Closure	

Friday 9th January:

TIME	TITLE	SPEAKER
9.00 a.m.	Registration	
9.15 a.m.	Introduction	Prof. Frank Convery, *Seminar Rapporteur.*
9.30 a.m.	Planning and Social Segregation in Dublin	Michael Bannon, *Department of Regional and Urban Planning, UCD.*
10.00 a.m.	The Role of the Planning Authority	Pat McDonnell, *Planning Section, Dublin Corporation.*
10.15 a.m.	Community and Environmental Services by Dublin Corporation, with special reference to Travelling People.	Christy Geoghegan, *Community and Environmental Section, Dublin Corporation.*
10.30 a.m.	Coffee/Tea	
11.00 a.m.	Open Discussion	
12.15 p.m.	Resumée	Professor Frank Convery, *Seminar Rapporteur.*
12.30 p.m.	LUNCH	
1.45 p.m.	Introduction & Contribution by Seminar Participants	Professor Frank Convery, *Seminar Rapporteur.*
3.15 p.m.	Coffee/Tea	
3.45 p.m.	Introduction to Panel Discussion by Professor Frank Convery	PANEL: Davy Byrne, *Assistant City and County Manager.* John Carroll, *Housing Administration, Dept. of Environment.* Pat McDonnell, *Planning Section, Dublin Corporation.* Paddy Morrissey, *Assistant City and County Manager.*
5.00 p.m.	Concluding Summary	Professor Frank Convery and Stanislaus Kennedy
5.15 p.m.	Closure of Seminar	

Participants at Focus on Homelessness Seminar, Dublin 1987

Ahern, Breda,
Balfe, Mark
Bannon, Michael
Barnes, Paul
Barnes, Queenie
Barrington, Ruth
Barry, Irene
Becker, Annalies
Blackwell, John
Blackwell, Jon M.
Boylan, Mary
Boyne, Peter
Brady, John
Brady, Vincent
Brophy, John
Browne, Mary
Buckley, Joe
Burns, Margaret
Byrne, Eric
Byrne, Liam
Byrne, Noreen
Byrne, Jane Dillon
Callaghan, Brian
Cantillon, John
Carroll, Bob
Carroll, Con
Cashman, Bob
Cassells, Peter
Cauley, John
Christopher, Sr.
Clare, Liam
Cogavin, Rose,
Collier, Rachel,
Coleman, Ursula
Collins, Martin
Collins, Michael
Convery, Frank
Cox, Olga

Creedan, Paula
Crickley, Stacia
Cronin, Joan
Crowe, Martin
Crowley, Flor
Cullen, Maura
Cullen, Rosemary
Cummins, Bernard
Cummins, Glen
Curley, Des
Curley, Margaret
Dalton, John
Daly, Afric
D'Arcy, D.P.
DeBarra, Cabrini
Deevey, Lena
Delaney, Deirdre
Deneher, Anna
Devit, Anne
Delaney, Phil
Delap, Charles
DeRossa, Proinsias
Doherty, Ger
Doherty, Michelle
Donnelly, Declan
Duignan, Eamon
Dunleavy, Clodagh
Dunphy, Jack
Dunne, Roisin
Editha, Joseph
Egan, Bernadette
Ennis, Mervyn
Fagan, Rita
Fannin, John
Farrell, K.
Fr. Farrell
Fay, Ronnie
FitzGerald, Garret

Fitzsimons, Karen
Ní Fhlatharta, Sheila
Flavin, E.
French, Ursula
Gavin, Michael
Geoghegan, Christy
Geoghegan, Feargal
Geoghegan, Philip
Geoghegan, Maureen
Gibbons, Siobhan
Gibbs, Sheila
Gleeson, Jack
Goodwin, Frank
Grant, Carmela
Greeves, Hughie
Gregan, Elizabeth
Halpin M.
Hanly, Hugh
Hanratty, Michael
Harkins, Bill
Harvey, Brian
Hegarty, Patricia
Helena, Sr.
Herron, Austin
Hickey, Julie
Higgins, Mary
Hilton, Grainne
Hogan, Jacinta
Hogan, Maria
Horkan, Mary
Hughes, Alfred
Hughes, M
Hyde, Niall
Hynes, Betty
Jackson, Lorraine
Jeffreys, Gerald
Jennings, Bob
Jennings, R

Jones, Anna
Joyce, Chrissey
Kane, Emer
Kane, M
Keane, Mary
Kearns, Peter
Keegan, M
Kelly, Mick
Kelly, Paul
Kelly, Riceal
Kelly, R
Kennedy, John
Kennedy, Stanislaus
Kenny, Brendan
Kenny, Brian
Kenny, Gerry
Kerrigan, M
Kirby, Mairead
Lambden, George
Lanagan, Catherine
Langstone, Valerie
Larkin, Lena
Larminie, Margaret
Lawless, Charlie
Lawlor, Catherine
Leahy, Alice
Lee, Anna
Leinster, John
Leonard, Elizabeth
Lynch, Carrie
Lynch, Gregg
Lynch, Ita
Lynch, Joseph
Lynch, Kathleen
Madden, Terry
Maher, Kathleen
Mangan, Sandra
Markey, Paula
Mason, John
McAleese, Mary
McBride, M.
McCabe, Carol
McCann, Michael

McCann, Tom
McCarthanagh, Ann
McCarthy, Donal
McCarchey, Pat
McCashin, Tony
McCautrey, Con
McCluskey, M.
McCormick, Mary
McCoughlin, M
McCourtney, Una
McCullagh, Joseph
McDaid, John
McDonnell, Pat
McDonnell, Seamus
McEnroe, J.
McGovern, Jim
McKeown, Sean
McLoughlin, Megan
McLoughlin, Ray
McMahon, Dermot
McNamara, P.
McNuillan, Bronagh
MacRiochaird, Connaill
McVille, Betty
Malone, David
Mooney, Olive
Mooney, Patricia
Moroney, Diarmuid
Morrissey, Paddy
Movnihan, J.
Muldoon, (Cllr) Mary
Mulkeen, Majella
Mulkrone, Ann
Mullaney, Charlie
Murphy, Ciaran
Murphy, Myles
Murphy, Patricia
Neville, Betty
Nolan, Joe
Norton, Mary
O'Boyce, Brian
O'Beirne, Paddy
O'Brien, Elizabeth

O'Brien, Justin
O'Brien, Thomas
O'Brien, M.
O'Connor, John
O'Donoghue, Gerry
O'Donoghue, John
O'Donoghue, Michael
O'Donnell, Geraldine
O'Driscoll, Breda
Ó Dúlacháin, Cormac
O'Grady, M.
O'Hargain, Sean
O'Keeffc, M.
O'Kelly, Caroline
O'Leary, Jimmy
O'Leary, Mick
O'Mahony, Denis
Ó Muire, Toal
Ó Siochrú, Emer
Ó Siochrú, Sean
O'Sullivan, Aidan
O'Toole, Tony
Owen, Aidan
Owen, Nora
Parker, Martin
Passe, John
Payne, M.
Phelan, Caroline
Pike, James
Poutche, S.
Power, Kathleen
Power, P.
Pritchard, Ann
Pryle, Fiona
Pugh, Morna
Rafferty, Michael
Reddy, Declan
Regan, Geraldine
Reville, Neil
Riordan, Noreen
Robbins, Joe
Rogerson, Pamela
Rooney, Maurice

Rotherford, Coleman
Rounaine, Tom
Ryan, Beryl
Ryan, F.
Ryan, Rita
Salmon, Fr.
Seery, Mark
Shannon, Dick
Sheridan, Betty
Sheridan, Shane

Steadman, Siobhan
Stewart, David
Sullivan, Chrissey
Stokes, P.
Susan, Sr.
Sweeney, John
Sweeney, Kevin
Sweeney, Owen
Sweeney, Pat
Synott, Mick

Taffe, John
Thompson, Bernard
Tighe, Irene
Treacy, M.
Watson, Brian
Webster, D.
Weir, Yvonne
Whelan, Mary
Whelan, Peter
Xavier, Sr.

Organisation Participation

Acra
Adult Education, Maynooth
AnCo
An Foras Forbartha
Aontas

Back Lane Night Shelter
Ballymun Leadership Course
Barnados
Brú Chaoimhín Hostel

Catholic Social Service Council
CentreCare
Cherish
Child Psychiatric Service (E.H.B.)
Clare County Council
Coolmine Assessment Centre
Commission on Social Welfare
Combat Poverty Agency
Comhlámh
Community Welfare Offices
Conference of Major Religious Superiors
Cork Corporation
Council for Social Welfare
Council for the Homeless
    (Northern Ireland)
Council of Travellers

Darndale Information Centre
Department of the Environment
Department of Health
Department of Social Welfare
Department of Justice
Dublin Central Mission
Dublin City Council
Dublin Corporation
Dublin County Council
Dublin Travellers Education and
    Development Group

Eastern Health Board
Economic and Social Research Institute
Exchange House

Fianna Fáil
Fine Gael
Focus Point
Free Legal Advice Centre
Friends of the Elderly

Galway Corporation
Galway Social Services
Gardiner Street Convent
Gingerbread

Holy Faith Convent, Finglas
Housing Centre

Institute of Theology and Philosophy
Interaid
Irish Foundation of Human
    Development
Irish Congress of Trade Unions
Irish Planning Institute

Kerry County Council
Kildare County Council

Labour Party
Limerick County Council
Laois County Council

Monaghan County Council
Mincéir Mislí
Meath County Council

National Association of Tenants
    Organisations (N.A.T.O.)
National Campaign for the Homeless
National Council for the Aged
National Council for Travelling People
National Economic and Social Council

National Rehabilitation Board
National Social Services Board
North Centre City Community Action
    Project (N.C.C.C.A.P.)
Northern Ireland Housing Executive

Open Door, Northern Ireland

Parents Alone
Percy Place
Prisoners Aid Through Community
    Effort (P.A.C.E.)

Rialto Parish Centre

Simon Community, Cork
Simon Community, Dundalk
Simon Community, Dublin
Simon Community, Galway
Simon Community National Office
Sheelin Homes
Social Service, Sherrard House
Stanhope Street Convent
St. Anne's Hostel

St. Brendans, MHA
St. Vincent's Centre
St. Patrick's College, Maynooth
South Inner City Community
    Development Association
SUSS
SUS Research

Tallaght Welfare Society
Threshold
Trust

Union of Students in Ireland
University of Dublin
University College Dublin

Waterford Corporation
Westmeath County Council
West Tallaght Resource Centre
Wicklow County Council
Workers' Party

Young Fine Gael
Youth Action Project, Ballymun

Agencies Referred to in this Book

Cherish is a single parent's association based on self-help, providing a drop-in centre, theraputic group work and information services to single parents in Dublin.

Dublin Travellers Education and Development Group is a voluntary group founded in 1983 and involves settled people and Travellers. The group is committed to the Travellers' right to self determination and equality in Irish society. It came together to develop alternative and innovative approaches to working with Travellers. The work is based on the premise that no lasting progress can be made unless Travellers themselves are facilitated to take control of their lives.

Focus Point is a self-help resource centre set up in 1985 providing various services and facilities to people out-of-home or stranded with nowhere to go. Its projects work together to provide a comprehensive settlement service for people out-of-home and socially vulnerable groups. These projects include:
— Information, advice and counselling
— Outreach streetwork
— Low cost restaurant
— Training
— Day Centre and Nursery
— Supportive short term housing
— Research Unit
— Outside Education Programme
— Settlement Service
— 24 Hour Phone In Service
— Education Service

South Inner City Community Development Association (SICCDA) established in 1982 to promote community development in the Liberties area of Dublin in a manner acceptable to and controlled by the local people themselves. The Association has eight sub-committees actively working on the following issues: the needs of the elderly, youth, planning and the environment, social action, training/education, sports/recreation, cultural and communications.

Threshold
Provides information, advice and practical assistance for people with housing problems. Specialised advice re problems in private rented accommodation, house purchase and local authority accommodation. Aims to tackle the problem of homelessness (lack of a secure, permanent place to live), provides an advisory service, research into housing deprivation and education programme.

Contributors

Michael Bannon lectures in Regional and Urban Planning at University College Dublin and carries out research consultancy work for regional development organisations. He is a member of the Irish Planning Institute and has worked as a consultant to the National Economic and Social Council and the Commission of the European Communities.

John Blackwell has carried out studies on population change, housing and social policy. He worked as a member of the Secretariat of the National Economic and Social Council and presently works in the Department of Environmental Studies, University College Dublin.

John Cauley is presently working as a Community Teamwork Supervisor with the Dublin Travellers Education and Development Group.

Michael Collins formerly was a supervisor on a Dublin Travellers Education and Development Group Community Teamwork Scheme (D.T.E.D.G.). Presently he works on a voluntary basis with D.T.E.D.G. and leads a drama group there.

Frank Convery formerly was a Professor in Duke University, North Carolina and research Professor of the Economic and Social Research Institute. Presently he is Heritage Trust Professor of Environmental Studies at University College Dublin.

Fred Donohue is presently Programme Manager of Community Care in the Eastern Health Board.

Mervyn Ennis has worked as a youth worker for the Dublin Committee for Travelling People and now works as a community worker with the Eastern Health Board in the south inner city of Dublin and works also with Travelling people in Dublin.

Christy Geoghegan is the Principal Officer of the Community and Environment Department of Dublin Corporation which provides a wide range of community recreational and environmental services for the people of Dublin. Included in his area of responsibility is the provision of accommodation for Travelling people in Dublin city.

Philip Geoghegan has been the consultant architect to the Iveagh Trust and has carried out a number of co-operative housing schemes in Ireland for the National Association of Building Co-operatives. Presently works as Director of the Housing and Urban Design Research Unit at University College Dublin.

Mary Higgins formerly Information Officer with Cherish. She presently works as Information and Education Officer in Emigrant Advice and is Chairperson of the National Campaign for the Homeless.

Stanislaus Kennedy R.S.C. is a Senior Research Fellow at UCD in the Department of Social Science, is a member of the Combat Poverty Agency and Co-ordinator of the Rural Projects of the EEC Programme to Combat Poverty. She is also founder and Director of Focus Point.

Thomas McCann recently completed a two year Community Development Course in St. Patrick's College, Maynooth. He is presently working with the Dublin Travellers Education and Development Group as a community youth worker with Travellers.

Pat McDonnell is Planning Officer with Dublin Corporation. He was in charge of preparation of the 1987 Dublin City Draft Development Plan.

Michael Mernagh O.S.A. formerly Director of a catechetical centre in Northern Nigeria and of the National Committee on Pilot Schemes to Combat Poverty. At present he works in Meath Street Parish and as advisor to the South Inner City Community Development Association and is responsible for the evaluation of its Social Action Project.

Paddy Morrissey is Housing Co-ordinator of the City and County of Dublin. Formerly he acted as Assistant City and County Manager responsible for Dun Laoghaire Corporation and Dublin County Council.

Justin O'Brien worked as child-care worker for six years and for Dublin Simon Community both as a full-time worker and as its Chairman. He was a social worker in Strathclyde, Scotland and is currently Settlement Officer in Focus Point, Dublin.

Cormac Ó Dúlacháin formerly worked as Director of Threshold and is now a member of its Executive Committee. Prior to that he was Development Officer for the Connemara West Project. Now he is practising Barrister at the Law Library, Dublin.

Aidan O'Sullivan presently works as the Housing Allocations Officer of the Dublin Corporation.

Michael Rafferty is Director of the North Centre City Community Action Group (N.C.C.A.P.) since 1978. He is actively involved at community level in major economic and social issues affecting the north inner city area of Dublin.

Dick Shannon joined National Simon Community in 1970 and has been Director of National Simon Community Ireland since 1974.

Chrissey Sullivan was member of a Dublin Travellers Education Development Group (D.T.E.D.G.) Community Teamwork Scheme. Presently she works as an assistant child care worker in a school for Travellers in Cork.

John Sweeney S.J. has worked in Latin America. Presently he is Director of the Jesuit Centre of Faith and Justice and is involved with various local community groups in Ballymun.

Bernard Thompson is currently employed as secretary of the National Association of Building Co-operatives (N.A.B.Co.) and is Chairman of the Housing Centre. He has been involved in housing organisations over the past 20 years.

West Tallaght Resource Centre is a project promoted by the Tallaght Welfare Society which engages in a range of social services. The project which uses a community development approach is directed at the problems of the residents of West Tallaght, with specific target groups being long-term and young unemployed people, welfare recipients, women who are isolated and single parent families.

By the same editors . . .

Who Should Care? The Development of Kilkenny Social Services. Stanislaus Kennedy RSC., Turoe Press, Dublin, 1981.

One Million Poor? The Challenge of Irish Equality. Ed. Stanislaus Kennedy RSC., Turoe Press, Dublin, 1981.

But Where Can I Go? Homeless Women in Dublin, Stanislaus Kennedy RSC., Arlen House, Dublin 1985.

Streetwise, Homelessness Among the Young in Ireland and Abroad, ed. Stanislaus Kennedy RSC., Glendale Press, Dublin, 1987.

Promise and Performance: Irish Environmental Policies Analysed, ed. John Blackwell and Frank J. Convery, Dublin, 1983.

Achieving the Revitalisation of Dublin:.What Works? ed. John Blackwell and Frank J. Convery, Dublin, 1988.

Replace or Retain? Policies Towards the Building Stock, ed. John Blackwell and Frank J. Convery, Dublin, 1988.

Other Focus Point productions . . .

Focus Point Directory and Guide to Social Welfare, Health, Housing, Legal Services and other Social Services in Dublin. Turoe Press, Dublin, 1985.

Foucs Point Guide to Supplementary Welfare Allowance and Districts in Dublin, Wicklow and Kildare. Who, Where, What and How of Supplementary Welfare Allowances, Focus Point, Dublin, 1986.

Nowhere To Go! The Challenge and Response to Homelessness in Ireland. Focus-Point Video Production, Dublin, 1986.

Focus Point in Focus. Dublin, June 1987.

Leaving Home Education Package. Focus Point, 1987.